Brian Wilson &
The Beach Boys

How Deep Is The Ocean?

*Essays & Conversations exploring the mysteries
of their incomparable musical accomplishments*

Paul Williams

OMNIBUS PRESS
LONDON · NEW YORK · PARIS · SYDNEY

Exclusive Distributors:
Book Sales Limited,
8/9 Frith Street,
London W1V 5TZ, UK.

Music Sales Corporation,
257 Park Avenue South,
New York, NY 10010, USA.

Music Sales Pty Limited,
120 Rothschild Avenue, Rosebery,
NSW 2018, Australia.

To the Music Trade only:
Music Sales Limited,
8/9 Frith Street,
London W1V 5TZ, UK.

Cover photo: LFI

Typeset by Galleon Typesetting, Ipswich.
Printed in Great Britain by Hartnolls Ltd, Bodmin, Cornwall.

A catalogue record for this book is available from the British Library.

Visit Omnibus Press at http://www.musicsales.co.uk

For information about Paul Williams's *Crawdaddy!* newsletter, visit
Cdaddy.com or write to Crawdaddy c/o Baldwin, 57 Tempsford, Welwyn
Garden City AL7 2PA UK, or write to Crawdaddy, Box 231155, Encinitas CA
92023 USA

Contents

this book is for
Cindy Lee Berryhill

Foreword
by David Leaf

When Paul Williams founded *Crawdaddy!* magazine over thirty years ago, he was one of a handful of American inventors of a new kind of rock music writing . . . supportive criticism that helped the ambitious artists of the day by letting them know that somebody out there was "getting" what they were doing.

Almost from the first issue, Brian Wilson and the Beach Boys were a regular subject in *Crawdaddy!*, and when Paul Williams wrote about Brian, it was with the kind of respect and awe that an artist of Brian's stature deserved. While that may seem self-evident in 1997, when Brian is revered for records like *Pet Sounds*, it wasn't quite that easy in 1967. Paul Williams wrote about Brian Wilson "in the moment," when Brian was the leading recording artist of the time, and he got it right. You can buy the *Good Vibrations* boxed set and hear what Brian did back then; read Paul Williams and you get a sense of what kind of person Brian was, and, remarkably, given everything he's been through, still is today.

Back in '67, Paul Williams was the leader of the pack who recognized Brian as an important composer/arranger/producer, one of the writers (Derek Taylor, et al.) who set the stage for the acceptance of *Smile* and the one whose post-mortem with Brian's A&R ace David Anderle may have shed more light on what *Smile* was to have been than all of the tens of thousands of words spilled on the subject since. While Paul Williams was not the first to put Brian "on paper" (publicist Earl Leaf first "created" the legend), he may be the one to have most influenced virtually all the writers who fell in love with the artist.

I first met Paul Williams in the late 1970s, but the impact of his writing has been a constant in my life for over a quarter of a century. Speaking just for myself, I know that the historical resonance in Williams' work was vital to what I've been able to write. I'm proud to say that he's become my friend, because what that means is that what I've written about Brian is okay with him.

That's not to say that Paul and I always agree. For example, I love *Orange Crate Art* much more than he does. That's not the first (nor I'm sure the last) time that our reaction to a record or a concert has differed, but as I've gotten to know Paul, I've realized it makes no difference. Because another great thing about Paul is that he almost welcomes disagreement with a spiritual calm, as if he knew that writing about music is, in many ways, art.

Paul is an artist who uses the written word to express passion – passion for what he loves. And in this case, on this particular subject, his passion, like mine, knows no bounds. So if Brian's music is about expressing emotion, as he once said, "under the guise of a record," then Paul Williams' writing is about doing the same thing – he writes from the heart . . . about how what he hears makes him feel.

And that feeling has produced an avalanche of words. In fact, just perusing the table of contents in this book is a trip. Reading the text itself is staggering – I'm amazed and impressed by the thirty years of work during which Paul Williams has written about Brian Wilson and his music in a way that is unlike anything else ever published. If you've never read Paul Williams but love Brian Wilson's music, you're in for a revelation. And if you think you've read Paul Williams, well, you might think again. I know that I found a lot of pieces here I didn't even know existed, and it's a true treat to have them all in one place now. Actually, the new material itself is worth the price of admission.

So join one of the few people for whom the phrase "rock critic" isn't an epithet, as he travels a remarkable personal journey, tracing thirty years of an artist's work in a grand celebration of the triumphs Brian (with and without the Beach Boys) has created for us all. Enjoy.

David Leaf

(David Leaf, a television writer and producer (*"You Can't Do That*: The Making of *A Hard Day's Night)*, is the author of the Brian Wilson biography *The Beach Boys & The California Myth* and the liner notes for the Beach Boys Capitol catalogue reissues.)

1

A Visit with Brian

I first got high on marijuana (not just smoked it but inhaled, got off) with Brian Wilson of the Beach Boys, in late December 1966. In a tent in his living room. I also first saw and used a videotape player and camera with Brian Wilson, in another part of that house. And heard wonderful, mysterious, unearthly music when he played *Smile* sessions acetates for me in another room. Stayed there that night, next day rode in a limo to a restaurant meal with Brian and the Boys and family members and others, followed by a trip to a recording studio where I recall lying on the floor with some Beach Boys in the semi-dark, making noises as instructed by our leader. All in two December days, the 23rd and 24th. It was fun. I didn't tell Lew Shiner this story before he wrote his novel *Glimpses*, but still he somehow managed to capture the exact *feeling* of my experience in the "boy visits Brian's house" segment of that novel.

I *was* a boy, eighteen, and Brian was very kind to me, very open and friendly. In a way he treated me as an equal, though he was six years older and a rich and successful recording artist. He vaguely knew I was the editor of this new sort of "underground press" rock and roll magazine, *Crawdaddy!*, and seemed comfortable with me recording our conversation (we called it an "interview") in the tent. We smoked grass or hash, in a hookah I guess. I wish I still had that tape (my grandfather had given me a small reel-to-reel tape recorder); all I can remember is that though I wanted a Brian Wilson interview for my magazine, when I got back to New York and listened to the tape there was nothing there that seemed like it would make sense or make sentences if I transcribed it. I do remember Brian telling me something about the history of bicycles, among other subjects. And I remember really liking the feeling of being in that tent, it was just like a small conference room, semi-luxurious, off to one side of the large living room. Having that thick, colorful fabric over us and around us was womb-like, pleasant, reassuring. I don't remember what the source of light was, but there was some. I think I slept in the tent, on pillows, that night.

While I was there that first afternoon (a cheerful fellow named Michael Vosse had come to my Hollywood motel – a dive chosen because my friends from back east the Youngbloods were also staying there – and driven me up to Brian's mansion on Laurel Way), a Christmas present arrived for Brian from Capitol Records. A big box. It was a Sony VideoTapeRecorder, not available in stores in the U.S. yet. Brian knew what to do. He called or had his wife call a technically competent cousin of theirs, a bright young man closer to my age than Brian's, who came over, read the instructions, connected the thing to a TV set and set up the camera. I guess he showed Brian which button to push. The cousin left, Marilyn went out if I'm remembering right, to get groceries or something, and Jules and Cissy Siegel came over. He was a journalist for the *Saturday Evening Post*, who later wrote of his friendship with Brian in the now-famous article "Goodbye Surfing, Hello God," published in October 1967 in the first issue of a new slick magazine edited by Siegel, *Cheetah*. She was later banned from Brian's mansion because Brian feared she was a witch.

We were in a sitting room with a sofa and chairs and a small Christmas tree set up on a table not far from the chairs. Brian or Jules turned on the camera and the TV set served as a monitor on which we could see what the camera saw, like closed-circuit TV. So we were seeing the room and one after another of us on this monitor, the camera turning easily, and then I remember vividly we were all four watching the screen, seeing the room on TV, and suddenly these little burn-holes began appearing in our reality, growing as we watched, burning. Jesus Christ! We quickly realized the lights on the Christmas tree were burning holes into the tape with their brightness, presumably because you weren't supposed to stop the camera while facing such small-but-intense light sources. Ooohhh, creepy. We turned off the camera. I think the Siegels had to go soon after that, but anyhow what I clearly remember is somehow Brian and I moved the camera and the monitor into another room (maybe Jules and Cissy helped before they left) and set them up facing a big stuffed armchair.

I sat in the chair at Brian's request; he asked me to talk so he could film me. I self-consciously kidded around about "here I am on this chair," and Brian was very appreciative. "This guy is so funny!" He laughed. "You are such a funny guy!!" He enjoyed making the tape. I didn't think I was so funny, but I liked being appreciated. When it was my turn to film him he was a little self-conscious, but anyway we tried out the new toy.

Marilyn came back, maybe with her sister Diane, fed the dogs, fed us a little later. I don't remember what else I did before Brian and I completed the night (it was quite late, two or four a.m., early morning of Christmas Eve day) by taking off our clothes and getting into the heated outdoor pool. But sometime that day, maybe more than once, Brian played me crumbling acetates of the music he'd been recording for the past couple of months. On a phonograph in his bedroom. And that of course was the cosmic purpose of the whole encounter. Like others – Jules Siegel, Tom Nolan, David Oppenheim for CBS, Richard Goldstein – I heard bits of the new music. The post-"Good Vibrations" music. Not songs but tracks, pieces of instrumental tracks, lovingly shared by Brian, and so hauntingly beautiful (except for the acetates that had already worn out) I couldn't forget them. I had to tell the world. We all did. Word got out. We were unconscious (and happy) instruments

13

of the historic process, of a legend that wanted to create itself. No hype. Good dope, yeah. But truly great music.

So at the end of the night we went to the pool, watched by the dogs. I kept my glasses on, because standing in that pool we could see the lights of Los Angeles (or the Valley) twinkling below us like a natural wonder. The water was warm. Brian told me enthusiastically that it was heated to exactly 98.6°, body temperature. "So if you get down in the water like this" (he demonstrated) "and stand up, it's like being born, like the feeling of being born." I appreciated his sense of wonder. A galaxy of stars seemed to be glittering below our mansion on the hill. It was four in the morning on the day before Christmas, and I was stoned for the first time (and this guy made me feel so at home). It was also the first time I'd been to California.

At some point, probably the next afternoon, I remember riding with Brian in a limo he had with grey-tinted windows, so you could see out but people couldn't see in. We went to a restaurant where we sat at long tables with a crowd of people including the other Beach Boys. I tagged along and tried to stay out of the way.

Later that day we went to a recording studio. I have two vivid memories of that part of my visit. One was Carl Wilson playing a 45 on a turntable somewhere in the studio. He'd just bought it and was eager to hear it because he had fallen in love with this record ("Gimme Some Lovin' " by the Spencer Davis Group) during the Beach Boys' recent visit to England. He talked it up to the assistant engineer who was helping him with the turntable, and then was horrified by what he heard. The American record company had remixed the song for American radio. And, to Carl's ears, had ruined its magic. He grabbed the record off the turntable, broke it over his knee and stomped on the pieces. And won my heart, since I was already a big fan of the (little-known) Spencer Davis Group. I just had to like this guy who cared enough about good music to get angry when it was fucked with.

14

The other memory, vivid but kinda fuzzy, is of Brian getting us to come into the large studio room where people usually play music, but he just wanted us to get down on the floor and make interesting noises, some kind of grunt. He demonstrated. It was kinda dark, with candles. I don't remember now if I actually grunted or just left that to the, um, professionals. Mostly I just remember the moodiness of being in that dark room, on the floor, hearing each other make these simple (but resonant) sounds. Gloriously weird. And then someone came to take me back to my motel, and my Christmas Eve visit with Brian and the Beach Boys was finished.

2

From the *Crawdaddy!* News Column, 1966–1967

In January 1966 I was 17, a freshman in college, and a DJ at the college radio station, and I had the idea that there should be a magazine about rock and roll, like the folk music magazines I'd been reading in my hometown, Cambridge, Mass. So I used a friend's mimeograph to publish what turned out to be America's earliest rock magazine, *Crawdaddy!* By May I'd dropped out of college, and by September I'd published the 5th issue of *Crawdaddy!* This was the first issue to include a news column (called "What Goes On?" from the Donovan song), and that column included the first words I think I ever wrote about the Beach Boys (although I'd been a fan of "Shut Down" and "I Get Around" for years), taken, like most of the news column, from what I read in the British music papers and the U.S. "trade" magazines, plus what I could hear with my own ears:

There seems to be some question as to which side is up on the BEACH BOYS' new single: "God Only Knows" is a smash in England; "Wouldn't It Be Nice" started big here but "God Only Knows" is catching up. Both are from <u>Pet Sounds</u>, the Beach Boys' finest LP. Their next LP should be called <u>Dumb Angel</u> (and watch for a number called "Good Vibrations"!).

And then the 7th issue (Jefferson Airplane on the cover) – dated January 1967 but off press in Dec. '66 before I met Brian

17

– mentioned the Beach Boys and Brian twice in the course of "What Goes On?":

"Good Vibrations" is the fastest selling Beach Boys single ever. No matter what you've heard, all the BEACH BOYS sing on "GV"; the instrumental work, however, is done by studio musicians. Some of the stranger sounds are from a theremin; now Brian wants a cathedral organ for the next album. ### BRIAN WILSON calls his next single, "Heroes and Villains," "a three-minute musical comedy, with some new production techniques that I think will surprise everyone." The next Beach Boys LP is now named Smile; nearly all the songs were written by Brian in collaboration with Van Dyke Parks, organist on many Beach Boys and Byrds tracks.

In the 8th issue (March 1967, Ray Davies on the cover, first review anywhere of Buffalo Springfield inside), I got wound up and delivered a sermon in the middle of "What Goes On?" that has at least some relevance to the subject of this book:

Something good is happening. Never mind Aaron Neville, Micky Dolenz, the bl**dy red baron or whatever else is on the radio. Go down to your friendly (maybe) record man and pick up the Doors album, the Youngbloods album, the new Stones, the new Donovan, the John Mayall Bluesbreakers LP (yes! yes! finally available in this country on London Records! You too can become an Eric Clapton fan), all of which came out in the last week as I write this. Never have there been so many great rock LPs out in one sudden spurt – never have there been so many different good things going on all at once – never have there been so many more good things promised for the immediate future. And this album activity comes at a time when we are just entering the millennium of performing rock, with college concerts replacing the teeny-bop bits, with the San Francisco scene beginning to spread across the country, with groups like the Airplane, the Springfield, Moby Grape, the Doors, who interact with

an audience and present live rock in a manner that cuts absolutely everything that has gone before. Everyone is getting into rock these days – and the only aspect of the scene that's going downhill is a.m. radio. The reason is obvious: a.m. radio, with its Monkees, its Herb Alpert, its Nancy Sinatra, is returning to the subteens from whence it came. Rock grew out of this, was born out of universality, popular appeal, the ability to sell a particular piece of material on a little 45 rpm disc. But the hard core audience for this kind of music is not a musical audience; they want pleasure, not interaction. Eventually the Beatles grew away from them, and the Monkees stepped in. It was inevitable – pop music is not based solely on creativity, and the people who don't interact had had it about up to here with creativity, new things every time you turned on the radio. It's not as easy to enjoy that stuff, particularly without really listening to it. So simple, bouncy, silly rock starts coming back and <u>somebody</u> is buying it. The beautiful part is: meanwhile rock has, through its growing goodness and through the graces of the generation that stayed with it, built up a huge audience for quality rock, creative rock, people who'd rather hear a good ten-minute rock track than an easy-to-listen-to, dull, catchy two-minute thing. These people know the difference between Question Mark & the Mysterians and the Buffalo Springfield, appreciate the aspirations of the Beatles and the Beach Boys, as well as the easy musicianship of the Youngbloods or the Spencer Davis Group. So we've come to that part of the circle where the top 100 is heading back towards formula, production tricks, reliance on catchy material, the whole bit. But we're getting off the circle, getting out of pop music, and we're taking a larger audience with us than ever before. We're getting into what all of us have been waiting for: a broad, creative music interacting with every facet of our world, reacting off of other kinds of music and more than that, other kinds of art, on a scale so large we can't even begin to guess at the consequences. But Brian Wilson must be the first composer in history to know that twenty million people are going to hear, and respond to, his new composition, within a month of his completing it. We are moving towards mass market creativity and interaction, and we're doing it in a context of media flexibility and a new awareness of man (look at San Francisco, where the new music first took hold). We are moving towards the audience-author relationship that made Shakespeare possible; and if you find out from the friendly record man that the Monkees have sold over five million albums, you just buy the Doors LP anyway, and play it with a couple of friends in a dimly lit room, and turn the transistor radio off and leave it off, 'cause that's not where we're going. ###

After that prophetic rave, I ended the March news column with a few brief bits, including:

The BEACH BOYS are forming Brother Records, and will try to get Capitol to release them from their contract ahead of time in exchange for distribution rights.

Next issue, May '67, the breaker between news items changed from ### to ::: , and this was the only BBs item:

::: The BEACH BOYS' suit against Capitol Records, which involves "replacement records deductions," is based on the theory that if you have a good enough lawyer you don't have to do anything you don't want to do; if this turns out to be true, a whole lot of people will stop doing what they don't want to do, which might even be nice. Tracks from the next Beach Boys LP include, "The Elements" (a composition in four movements), "Heroes and Villains" (their next single, weighing in at over four minutes), "The Child Is the Father of the Man" and something about going in the yard to eat worms. Lyrics are mostly by Van Dyke Parks, and it is possible that the LP will be finished one of these days. Smile. :::

Crawdaddy! 10, Aug. '67: ::: Good news: CARL WILSON has been cleared of draft-dodging charges against him; he still has not achieved the C.O. status he deserves, however. It is unclear at this point when the Beach Boys will release Smile, or any new album; there are too many conflicting reports. Let's hope that Brian will not fall into the trap of becoming so enamored of perfection that he produces nothing rather than produce the imperfect (even though he may be six times better now, the work he did last December is more deserving of release than 99.44% of what's available by anybody else). :::

And this related item: ::: "Donovan's Colours" by George Washington Brown (VAN DYKE PARKS) is now available on a Warner Brothers 45. It's two years ahead of its time, and required listening for *Crawdaddy!* people. :::

Okay, #11, Sept./Oct. '67, is the issue with a cover photo of Paul McCartney taken by our staff photographer, Linda Eastman, the day she first met her future husband. In "What Goes On?" in #11, I had this to say about the BBs and related topics:

::: Lance Fent has left the PEANUT BUTTER CONSPIRACY and is replaced on lead guitar by Bill Wolff. The group has high hopes of dumping Gary Usher and recording a good LP. : Gary Usher is a producer for Columbia on the west coast, who works with the Byrds and Chad & Jeremy. He was a friend of Brian Wilson's and a bank teller when Brian collaborated with him on some songs and brought him into the music world. Interestingly enough, it was a record produced and arranged by Gary Usher, called "My World Fell Down," which – because of similarities between "My World Fell Down" and Smile tapes that Brian had stored under lock and key at Columbia's Studio D in Los Angeles – caused Brian Wilson to stop using professional studios and instead build a four-track recording studio in his new home. Much of the BEACH BOYS' Smiley Smile was probably recorded there. : Smiley Smile, by the way, is not the same album as the much-anticipated Smile. The latter was to be a full collaboration with Van Dyke Parks, and would have included "Surf's Up," "The Child Is the Father of the Man," and "The Elements" (a four-part evocation of earth, air, fire and water), among others. What happened to it? The gap between conception and realization was too great, and nothing satisfied Brian by the time he'd worked it out and gotten it on tape. And eventually the moment passed – if <u>Smile</u> could have somehow been kidnapped in January of 1967 and released as an unfinished work, the world would be considerably richer. But like many other fine artists before him, Brian was unable to realize his original concept of <u>Smile</u> when he wanted to, and after a while he no longer wanted to. He no longer had the same vision. Most of those tapes have reportedly been destroyed; anyone who ever heard any of the achingly beautiful tracks laid down for <u>Smile</u> must be deeply saddened by that news. Very few growing artists like what they did six months ago – which doesn't mean it isn't good, of course. Brian got to a state where – because he grew so fast – he couldn't stand last week's stale genius, he had to forge ahead. And <u>Smiley Smile</u> . . . Like "Heroes and Villains," it could no longer be a perfect work, so it might as well be whatever it was. ("Heroes and Villains" originally had a chorus of dogs barking, cropped when Brian heard <u>Sergeant Pepper</u>, and was in many ways – the bicycle rider – a far different song). <u>Smile</u> is the one that got away. :::

3

Outlaw Blues (*Beach Boys Party!*)

This was written in December 1967 as part of a Crawdaddy! *essay that also included long discussions of the Rolling Stones'* Their Satanic Majesties Request *and Jefferson Airplane's* After Bathing at Baxter's. *The essay was called "Outlaw Blues," after the Dylan song that the thought that opens and closes the essay was taken from. It became the title chapter of my first book.*

"I wish I was on some Australian mountain range . . ."

People who work in mass media are supposed to be half manipulator and half prophet; and all around the mulberry bush now producers, performers, and persons who just like to rap are wondering about the Future of Rock (and roll). They talk about stuff like the following:

During 1967 rock music, thanks to Beatles Doors Airplane etc., greatly expanded its audience to the point where maybe two-thirds of the people buying any records at all were buying rock albums. Meanwhile, also thanks to Beatles Doors Airplane etc., the number of creative musicians and groups within the field grew even faster. Situation: during the summer of 1967, by some awesome coincidence, the size and interests of the buying audience coincided nicely with the quantity and quality of rock albums newly available to them, and hence the considerable success of people like Jimi Hendrix, Country Joe & the Fish, the Doors, the Mothers, Moby Grape, and so on. Lots of creative people making it pretty big with creative stuff, and this in turn led to unrestrained enthusiasm on the part of large record

23

companies, who've been spending unbelievable amounts to make sure that any group that sounds talented to them will in the future record on their label. In the same manner, successful groups have pushed and shoved their way into the studios, sparing no expense, taking as much time and using as many tools as might seem necessary to really Do What They Want To Do. Because it looks like the enthusiasm of the audience for good stuff will make it all worthwhile.

But already in December 1967 the difficulties are becoming apparent. For one thing, there are quite a number of good groups making records, and they all expect a slice of the pie. Can the same audience that – phenomenally – put the Beatles, the Doors, the Stones, and Jefferson Airplane in the top five on the LP charts at the same time, can they purchase enough records now to put Donovan, Love, Country Joe, Judy Collins, the Rolling Stones, the Beatles, the Beach Boys, Van Dyke Parks, the Hollies, Paul Butterfield, Jefferson Airplane, the Incredible String Band and Buffalo Springfield in the top five at the same time? All of the above have released new albums in the last month, as I write this, and the Who, the Kinks, Moby Grape, the Byrds, Jimi Hendrix, Randy Newman, the Grateful Dead, the Mothers, and the Velvet Underground have stuff scheduled for the immediate future. Elbow room! cried Dan'l Boone. Every one of these groups expects to be able to spend $50,000 or more recording an album, and if this much good stuff is going to be released every two months, who's going to pay for it?

The immediate answer is clear: expand the audience. But since we've already moved in on most of the existing music audience, this means a very heavy undertaking: we have to increase the number of people who are actually listening to and buying any music at all. We have to not only show why rock music is good music, but why Music Itself Is Good For You and so on and on. And maybe even the quantity of really good stuff being released nowadays will help us do it.

But there's one word back there you might have overlooked:

coincidence. What if it suddenly turns out that what Country Joe & the Fish (or even the Beatles) feel like doing with all that expensive recording-time freedom is not the same thing as what our dear expanding audience wants to listen to? What if good creative art is not always appreciated by huge numbers of people the instant it's available?

That's What People Are Talking About, folks. And it's all fairly relevant to the albums at hand. The Beach Boys, a group that class prejudice prevents many of us from appreciating, released in the summer of 1966 an album called *Pet Sounds,* to me one of the very finest rock albums of all time. It was not exactly Far*Out, but it was kinda subtle compared to the previous Beach Boys stuff; and partly for that reason, and mostly because of timing, *Pet Sounds* was the first Beach Boys album in several years not to be a million-seller. The timing factor was one not unfamiliar to us in 1967 – the big hit on the album, "Sloop John B," made it in December 1965, but because of the amount of studio time required to do the album right, *Pet Sounds* wasn't released till June and lost its impact as a result. And the mere fact that the record was really beautiful wasn't enough to salvage the situation. The public doesn't always care about that.

But the public *loved* the group's previous album, *Beach Boys Party!,* a million-seller which most of us heavy rock listeners looked down upon as a sloppy, drunken recording of moldy oldies from 1961. Not even good (we thought then) in the context of The Beach Boys, let alone as a Rock Album. Yet the record sold terrifically, despite its dollar-extra price (a gala gatefold presentation), and the fact that there was another Beach Boys album, released just before it, competing for the fans' attention.

So maybe Beach Boys record-buyers are stupid, and we can dismiss the whole thing. But maybe that's a pretty snotty attitude to take; maybe something is happening here that we just ought to know about. *Beach Boys Party*! is an excellent album containing excellent music *that is easy to relate to*!! And

25

that's why the public dug it, dug it more than that other excellent LP *Pet Sounds*, and that's the real reason people buy records – not because they're dupes, but because they like music, and the better it is the more they like it as long as they are still able to relate to what's good about it.

Not that I want to say that if lots of people like something, it's good. We all know what Humpty Dumpty said, and since I'm the one who's stuck with whatever definition of the word I care to accept, I'll feel more comfortable believing it's "good" if I feel it is, rather than it's "good" if it wins the popularity polls. But we are talking about the relationship between what a performer feels like doing and what a large audience – large enough to pay for that performer's studio time – feels like listening to. So the extent to which large bunches of people are able to relate to things is pretty important.

I said the *Beach Boys Party!* album is excellent, and I was talking about my own subjective response, of course. Yet that's an educated response – i.e., in 1965 I didn't like the record, I really put it down, and now after two more years of listening to rock intensively I feel that the album is a very good one. My opinion now is probably more valid than my opinion then – not because of any directionality of time but because I'm writing for an audience of people most of whom have also listened to a great deal of rock in the last two years. They can relate to my present point of view, at least in terms of common experience.

Let's drop this for a moment. Do you like the new Stones album? I hope you do. I went through a period of about a week (after loving it initially) where I was really unsure if I liked it or not.

[The essay continues, revealing that "now I am quite convinced it's a great record" and going into much detail about the pleasures of *Their Satanic Majesties Request.* This is followed by a close look at another album I was very taken with in

12/67, *After Bathing at Baxter's* by Jefferson Airplane. I swerve back to the subject of the Beach Boys after this comment on "Won't You Try," the last track of the Airplane album: "If you're in any kind of good spirits, this song will raise them through the roof. And isn't that what we really want from rock music?"]

That's what we get from the Beach Boys. *Beach Boys Party!* is a friendly, pleasant record, recorded by people who really understand the common ground between "Papa-Ooom-Mow-Mow," "Mountain of Love," and "The Times They Are A-Changin'." "It's *all* rock," as R. Meltzer or anybody would say, and the Beach Boys really know what that means. It means this is music that's "here for you any old time," and that means you if you're a performer pleasantly fooling around at a party, or you if you're a kid camping out at Big Sur with a portable phonograph and a copy of "Light My Fire."

And you've got to give the Beach Boys credit (especially if you don't want to). Because this album was recorded two and a half years ago, and it's full of the sort of understanding that most rock performers are just beginning to get into. Street noises were nice before John Cage put his signature on them; and what's the difference if the Beach Boys really *had* a party, and the Stones just pretended to have one?

I mean, I'm talking about the perception of things. It's all in how you see it. In *Crawdaddy!* 11 we ran a centerfold of Jim Morrison, "Cancel My Subscription to the Resurrection." It was sort of designed as a poster, but we didn't indicate that in the magazine, because we thought it might sound silly. So a lot of people thought it was a paid ad. Then Jefferson Airplane sent us a thousand dollars, and a two-page ad of group doodling related to their new album. We ran it as a centerfold in number twelve, and naturally it looked like copy; it didn't look like an ad at all. But so what? Both spreads were quite attractive, and does it really matter *which* one brought in some cash to help put out the following issue?

What's important is that our readers enjoyed this stuff. Maybe even got something out of it, on a personal level. And what matters in music is what's there, what's audible and recognizable and "meaningful" in any way whatsoever to the person listening (and to the people playing). Intentions, motivations, circumstances . . . those are for historians. They're interesting, nice to know about, useful and even important, but they don't have to do with the music and the immediacy of listening to it.

And context notwithstanding, the thing that makes *Beach Boys Party!* a good album (to me) is the fact that it's nice to listen to. But what makes it an excellent album is that while I'm listening to this record-that-is-nice-to-listen-to, I get a lot of extra stuff: I get moved on an emotional level, I get insight into the nature of rock music and the creative impulse itself, I get impressions of the world and the way people feel about it, I get a lot of just plain good reactions. Stuff that stays with me. And at no added cost, which kind of makes this record better than just any nice-to-listen-to album.

And the same is true of the Stones and Airplane albums, and lots of other stuff. The Beach Boys deserve historical credit for understanding and expressing something (a certain attitude toward music) first, but the value of the record *now* has nothing to do with when it came out. And it's obviously not necessary to read this review in order to appreciate any of these records. It might be nice to listen to some stuff after getting a really detailed look through another person's eyes (ears), but that's a different pleasure. I wrote a whole article in *Crawdaddy!* 11 about the aspects of listening to rock in a particular environment, the extent to which the context can be part of the musical experience. Groovy. Now I want to make it as clear as can be that the *creation* of the music is non-contextual, that we've gone beyond the days when rock was specifically designed for everybody's car radio. The musician, the performer, can *not* create music for people in other recording studios, who also have Altex 605 speakers, or whatever, to listen through. He (or she) can't become involved only in what his own ears perceive, at the moment of creation and the playback five minutes later.

Or rather, he certainly can. I correct myself. I'd be the last person to urge restrictions on anyone's freedom, and I sincerely believe that creating for an audience of ten, or one, or zero, is just as valid as anything else. Certainly the quality of something is not measured by multiplying it by the number of people who dig it.

But what I'm really talking about, of course, is that old coincidence. I'm talking about the performer who expects to spend as much money on recording time and engineers and instruments and whatever as is needed to do what he wants to do. No matter how you divide up the wealth of the world, there is not at the present time sufficient time-money-energy on Earth to give every person alive an engineer, a set of musicians, all the instruments he or she wants and five weeks of time in a well-equipped studio. So anyone who wants all those privileges had better either be a fascist, or a person who is creating for more than a half dozen people. Because if people will pay for these records that cost so much to make, fine. If you want to spend all that money making the music, and they're willing to spend all that money to listen to it, nothing could be fairer.

But beware the coincidence. I've spent a lot of time in this article trying to get at some of the reasons *why* people are willing to buy what the Stones, the Airplane, and the Beach Boys are trying to do. Why people enjoy the stuff, what they get out of it. What makes it all worthwhile. There are a lot of records I couldn't justify as well. Some of these records cost a lot of money (and I'm not talking about dollars, I'm talking about people, and the time spent by people other than the artist on all the aspects of this process, including earning the "money" to support the process). And some of the artists who made these records are beginning to think they have a God-given right to take up as many people's time as they want in order to do their thing. Jabberwocky!

Beware the baldersnatch, my son. Beware the confusion that comes at the top, that comes from thousands of people waiting for your new album, that comes from record companies standing in line for the right to spend money on you, that comes from fourteen-page magazine articles about how great you are. Remember you are only you, remember that your prime concern should be doing what is most important to you, but that you have a responsibility, a very real responsibility, to every person other than yourself who gets involved in the achieving of your personal goals.

That doesn't mean hey sing "White Rabbit" for us, Grace. No, the point is not to think that you have any responsibility to anybody because they've bought your records or whatever they did in the past. The point is to think about the present, think about whether what you're doing is worth whatever is going into it. Because, forgetting the morality of the thing, what happens to our creative artists if nobody buys their new albums and they have to go back to recording in a garage?

Rock music is the first good music in quite a while to achieve a mass acceptance. It is also one of the few really worthy side-effects of the current state of mass media in the Western world. Because many rock musicians, rock producers, rock etcetera do not appreciate the significance of this, we are in serious danger right now of blowing the whole bit. With the best intentions in the world, the ideal of serving pure art and pure individual creative instinct, we may drive ourselves out of the recording studio and the mass media and back into our garages and audiences of half a dozen friends. If we don't try our damnedest to make music that is both of high quality *and* accessible to a fairly widespread audience, we may look pretty silly a year from now complaining that no one pays us any attention.

But I don't want to end on a polemical note. Why, it might

cut down the pleasure value of my own creating! And anyway, I think Ray Davies must be the only person ever to have written a song entitled "There's Too Much on My Mind."

"I got no reason to be there, but I imagine it would be some kind of change."

4

A Celebration of *Wild Honey*

This was written in January 1968 as an introduction (and amendment) to the first installment of perhaps the most unusual and best-received essay about music I ever "wrote," my interview with David Anderle about Brian Wilson, published as "Brian" in Crawdaddy! *(March, May, and June 1968) and as the centerpiece to my first book,* Outlaw Blues. *(See chapters 5 and 6.) I wrote "A Celebration of* Wild Honey *" two months after the conversation included in this book as chapter 5.*

When David Anderle and I began our discussion of Brian Wilson, we had just finished listening to *Wild Honey* (The Beach Boys, Capitol Records, November 1967) for about the second time. We were depressed. We both count ourselves among the World's Most Loyal Brian Wilson Fans – David worked with Brian and the Beach Boys in 1966–1967, as a friend, as an advisor in the realm of business, as the head of Brother Records (the Beach Boys' own record cornpany) – but we just couldn't see *anything* in this new album. This is reflected in our comments throughout the interview.

I haven't talked with David, but I'm sure he's changed his mind. *Wild Honey* is one of last year's finest albums, a lovely record full of exuberant singing and beautiful, evocative music. The best that can be said for the lyrics is that they don't get in the way (though they are masterfully inappropriate at times). The instrumentation and overall sound are crude as can be – the record was no doubt recorded in

Brian's home studio. But very few things can stand in the way of really fine music, and this record is the triumph of the creative musician over the incredible hassles of the music world.

Hooray!

• • •

I'm just sitting and thinking, pulling things together. I wouldn't dream, at this point, of trying to do a significant article on Paul Williams; I know nothing about him. And yet I've somewhere got the idea that I can write about the Beach Boys. Fun, Fun, Fun. God Only Knows. The Beach Boys relate to my very core, little else; can I write about that?

I came across the Beach Boys when I was most alone. Not lonely, I don't mean that; but no one listened to my albums. Music was part of my most private world: Harvard Square after 1 A.M., walking the sides of highways, New York a day at a time, *Blonde on Blonde* late into the afternoon and later. No one talked to me about music; people talked to me about the magazine and the weather, when they talked at all. But Derek Taylor wrote an article in *Hit Parader*, and Al Kooper at Newport mentioned *Pet Sounds* as his favorite record, and "God Only Knows" sounded good on eight transistors, and eventually I bought the album. Eagerly and reluctantly. After all, the Beach Boys?

The Beach Boys. In a week, *Pet Sounds* was my closest friend. Even today only *Pet Sounds*, "If Only We Knew" (John Handy), and "Sad-Eyed Lady" can really calm my nerves. Walking sandy shores. I don't know what I find in this music, but it's always there: warmness, serenity, friendship. Strength. I decided *Pet Sounds* was the best rock album yet with no advice from anyone, and I never changed my mind. At some point a person sets up his own aesthetic standards, which can't be justified, can't be questioned; I began this process for myself with *Pet Sounds*. It doesn't have reasons, it's a starting point. Foundation stone. A few decisions shape our lives.

• • •

Celebration. *Smile* is the album that never was, and *Smile* is the reason that David and I were slow to respond to *Wild Honey*. We expected more. We expected more, in fact, than we would expect from any other composer alive, because the tracks we'd heard from *Smile* were just that good. *Smiley Smile* was the record put out instead of *Smile*, when that fell through; a confusion, a record with a few of *Smile*'s songs, changed around quite a bit, but almost none of the tracks recorded for the earlier album. And *Wild Honey* is just another Beach Boys record, which is only to say that it's not *Smile*, and it was necessary for us to forget *Smile* before we could appreciate what came later.

Well, no. *Smile* is not forgotten, never will be. But I am comfortable with *Wild Honey* now, love *Wild Honey* now, because it is new and fresh and raw and beautiful and the first step in the direction of even greater things than what was once to be. I celebrate *Wild Honey* as a work of joy, and one more gift of music from probably the most creative musician alive. I celebrate *Wild Honey* for "Country Air," for "I'd Love Just Once to See You," for "Aren't You Glad," for "Darlin' " . . . for all this music that is so listenable and so moving and so very very original and good on the level of what I believe music really is. I celebrate *Wild Honey*.

Hooray!

5

How *Smile* Got Lost

This conversation (parts I & II) was recorded at the end of November, 1967, in Laurel Canyon, Hollywood. The speakers are David Anderle and Paul Williams.

I

PAUL: Why don't we start off from the – DAVID: Crying. PAUL: Crying? [laughter] DAVID: Where would you like to start? PAUL: I guess we might as well start from how difficult this album makes it, and then just take it back and see what happens. DAVID: Okay. In a way, it doesn't make it as difficult as *Smiley Smile* did, because *Smiley Smile* was closer to the stuff that he cut for the original *Smile* album. PAUL: It's easier to forget this one. DAVID: Right. But you can't forget *Smiley Smile*, if you were around when Brian was cutting the stuff for the original *Smile*.

It's very hard to listen to this album, *Wild Honey*, and figure out what . . . there's so much that could cause that, it's difficult to really ascertain, not seeing Brian for a while, what it could be. The fact of his trying to cut in his own house I think has a lot to do with it, 'cause that's limiting him. I think the major problem from *Pet Sounds* to this album is, um, the fact that the Beach Boys, the Beach Boys number one as a musical instrument and the Beach Boys always being negative towards Brian's experimentation. They were generally very aware of

37

the commercial market, when Brian really wanted to space out and take off, and would've been the first . . . "I Am the Walrus" [brand new Beatles single the week of this conversation], for instance. Brian was doing Hawaiian chants, we used to lay around the house a year and a half ago, a year ago, a bunch of us, and do Hawaiian chants and all kinds of chanting, and all kinds of animal noises. Everything that's being done now that I hear, it's like old hat – it's like laying around Brian's house. But then he would go through some kind of a number waiting for the guys to return, because he knew that they would balk at that kind of experimentation at that point. They wanted to stay pretty much within the form of what the Beach Boys had created – really hard . . . whatever that is, California rock or whatever.

It's a very hard thing to explain. For instance, Brian could cut a whole album like *Pet Sounds* by himself. Which is why, I think, that Brian is really the foremost person in rock music. The ability for him to sit down, at a piano, and write a song, and take it into the studio, and not only produce it but engineer it, control the board, know exactly what he wants to do, play almost any of the instruments he wants to play, chart it himself, uh, and sing all the parts! Had he been able to do that, and do it today, you wouldn't have a *Wild Honey*, I don't think. I don't think you would have a *Smiley Smile*. You would have had the *Smile* that you heard some parts of, that are still sittin' around somewhere, that's got to be one of the great albums of all time, if it ever comes out.

Other than that, I really don't know why *Wild Honey* is there. It's so naked compared to what he has in him. And he can't lose that. A person like Brian cannot *lose* what he has. Now maybe mentally he could be off into another thing, 'cause Brian has a tendency to get into things, you know, he gets all that fantastic energy, that, uh, I don't like to use the word "genius," but he gets that fantastic Brian Wilson thing into a direction and it's like, everyone watch out, it's like a tank moving through wheat, and he'll go until he gets bored. Not *tired,* 'cause Brian never gets tired, but when he gets bored, immediately it's off and he's onto another direction. I don't know what direction this is. At all. This is no direction . . . it's almost pacification, it's almost giving up. You really get a feeling that Brian is either tired, or he's given up, or he just doesn't give a shit. It could be, perhaps, that he just doesn't give a shit at this point.

PAUL: What happened to the record company, to Brother Records? DAVID: Brother Records is very close and dear to my heart. At the time that I left, or that Brian and I parted company on a business level, officially, whatever, Brother Records was just in the formation stages. Brother Records was really a dream that Brian had, a nonbusiness concept that I somehow in a series of very long conversations over a long period of time, tried to show Brian how to structure it. Hence, when it was time to get serious, my function was to be head of Brother Records, which was exactly that, either head or chief. There were no titles. It was gonna be the first real non-uptight, positive, youth company, record company [Apple Records was not launched until six months after this conversation, more than a year after Brother Records began], and all our juices were directed in that direction. We were going to do things that had never been done before. There were not going to be any weirdnesses like you run into in the record business right now.

But it can't be that way. As long as you have to maintain a business that deals with the distributors, for instance, or the people who can't get on your trip, then somehow you have to compromise, and somehow you have to play a little of their game. Brian was totally uncompromising. And probably, had I been crazy enough at that time, and given Brian the total strength that I should have given to him, we could have done it, 'cause Brian can really do anything he says he's gonna do. There's just no question of that.

Well, we got Brother Records going. The first thing we had to do was sever the relationship with Capitol Records. Uh . . .

Brother Records was not really formed so that the Beach Boys could make more money; Brother was formed so that Brian could have more free direction. Which doesn't look like that's happening. I mean this is the great paradox, it looks like he's tied more now than he was before. It could be the restrictions of having his own label, maybe . . . PAUL: Well, *Wild Honey* has been released on Capitol . . . DAVID: And I have no idea why that is. When I was told that *Wild Honey* was coming out on Capitol, I tried to search in my head, one, what kind of an agreement they could have made . . . PAUL: Maybe Brian thinks, if it comes out on Capitol, it doesn't count. DAVID: That's very good. That's very good, 'cause Brian has a naive streak running through him which is really beautiful, and you wish you could hop onto that naive thing. Brother Records was like a precious little oasis; it was going to have only those things that Brian was in love with.

I left because at the time that *Smile* was being done, it was impossible to run Brother Records as a business. No decisions could be made. Brian at that time got his head out of the business thing completely and into the studio, and then got his head completely out of anywhere; we couldn't find where his head was at for a whole long period of time. And operating a business without being able to get decisions from Brian just wouldn't work. So I moved out. A lot of us moved out. I really don't know that much about Brother at this point, except what I see, and what I see is not really that happy.

PAUL: Let's try to trace the history of *Smile*, from *Dumb Angel* [Brian's original name for the album] or even earlier; in fact, why don't we start with the origins of *Pet Sounds*, however much you know, and just go right through? DAVID: Fine. Okay. The origins of *Pet Sounds* . . . At one point I came into the Beach Boys' lives, or into Brian's life, right around the *Beach Boys Today* and *Beach Boys Concert* albums. PAUL: March '65. DAVID: Right, somewhere around there – I came in through a relative of mine who was a friend of a few of the Beach Boys and then I was out again. And then I was brought

40

up to Brian's house one night, a long time ago, and we just hung out for a while, and it was very groovy. I really liked Brian right away, I liked him because there was something there, that I had not seen in many people in my lifetime. And I was out again. The people in Brian's life are very much in and out, in and out; you're around for a while, and then you're gone, because of Brian's . . . the thing I mentioned earlier, the fact that Brian gets into something so intently and then he's out of it and he goes into a new thing, and if you personally can't get into the new thing then either you have to go by yourself or they make it known, on a very non-uptight level, that you're just not fitting in.

When I really got in with Brian was right around the time of the fourth, final "Good Vibrations" [summer '66]. I heard it, and it knocked me out, and I said, uh oh, there's something happening here that is unbelievable. And then, the next time I came up, it was different. And the next time I came up it was different again. And then I came up one evening, and Brian said – at that time I had left MGM, and I was managing an artist named Danny Hutton, who is now recording for Brian – Brian informed me at that time that he had decided to totally scrap "Good Vibrations." He was not going to put it out. The track was going to be sold to Warner Brothers to be put out as an r&b song, sung by a colored group. Brian has always had a feeling for r&b, *very* heavy feeling for r&b. So I went home, I talked to Danny and Danny said, well, let's work out a deal, let's see if I can't record the song and have Brian produce it and finish it and the whole thing. I called Brian back the next day and I proposed, made a proposal to him, which I don't personally think caused him to decide to finish, but maybe he . . . it gave him a different perspective. Anyway, he went ahead and he finished it.

PAUL: What was the nature of the earlier "Good Vibrations"? DAVID: It was a lot shorter, it was a lot tighter rhythmically, melodically it was a lot simpler than the final song. It was much more a commercial ditty, if that's possible. There were

41

no lyrics at that time, that he had recorded; he had just recorded tracks. Brian goes in and cuts all the tracks first. He is motivated by the music, generally; the music will then motivate the lyric, and a lot of times the lyric comes very late. Brian is totally musical. Obviously he's not lyrical. Brian has written some of the worst lyrics in history. Although you shouldn't say "worst" lyrics, but some of the simplest lyrics. His lyrics have never been on the par that his music has been on, ever. He really has a musical head.

PAUL: "Sloop John B." ended up an integral part of *Pet Sounds*, and really fit; but was it created before the rest of the album? DAVID: Oh yes. PAUL: I understand it was an attempt to give the Beach Boys a virile image, a masculine image. DAVID: Well, at that time they had started getting hit, the whole hippie thing had started. You remember, now the hippie thing is coming, the underground is starting to bubble up for the first time. PAUL: *Revolver*. DAVID: Right. The Beatles have done *Revolver*, uh, Dylan is popular, Dylan is a big thing, Dylan was a big thing for Brian. He had a very big thing going for Bob Dylan. He thought Bob Dylan was . . . ha, very amusingly . . . he felt that Dylan was placed in the music scene to end music. He thought that musically he was very destructive, although lyrically . . . interestingly enough, if you go back, one of the few songs that Brian has ever recorded on an album that has not been a Brian Wilson song is a Bob Dylan song, they recorded a Bob Dylan thing ["The Times They Are A-Changin' "] on the *Beach Boys Party!* album. PAUL: Great album. DAVID: Right! PAUL: Now there's one that will eventually get credit for being a first. DAVID: And that album has the feeling – PAUL: Of the Stones' LP [*Their Satanic Majesties Request*, just released]. DAVID: Right, that has that whole, beautiful laying-around-the-house, doing-a-number . . . PAUL: And with the musical integrity. DAVID: Way ahead of its time.

Brian was taking a great deal of slamming at that time from the heavy critics about them being, you know, "wimp rock," and "ball-less rock," and "high school sopranoes" and the whole number. There were very few people who recognized the genius of Brian Wilson. So he wanted to get into that a little bit, and then he also got into some mind-expanding ventures that allowed him to really sit back and hear things for the first time. He himself personally was going through some changes; he became very interested in Subud, then moved on into astrology, numerology, occult . . . Brian is a fantastic reader, this is another thing people don't understand. If people would take time to talk to him . . . 'Cause he doesn't talk, he's nonverbal, he's a nonverbal human who reads intently, reads some of the heaviest material and instantly knows exactly what's going on. Somebody tried to lay the *I Ching* on him for a period of time – he had the whole thing psyched out, if that's possible, he had the thing psyched out immediately. Now again, his study of numerology, and Subud, and all the occult was not what you would call normal, it was so far more intent than man is supposed to go. I mean he really gets into it, to such a point that when you're with him, at five o'clock in the morning, and you're laying around and he's discussing certain things with you that you absolutely want not to believe, he forces you to believe them, with an incredible amount of knowledge of the subject, and then a tremendous amount of perception. The most perceptive man I've ever met is Brian Wilson.

Anyway, all this was going on at the same time, this is all happening now and he's starting to meet people . . . who are not from Hawthorne, California. He's starting to meet other people who are into different areas of, uh, academic study, or intelligentsia, and they're starting to lay numbers on his head, and Brian is like eating all this up, as he always does. Then he gets into *Pet Sounds*. *Pet Sounds* was a very long project, it was the cutting of a whole bunch of tracks, which is his pattern, same pattern as *Smile*, going in and getting an idea, going in and putting it down, putting it away, doing something else, putting it down, putting it away, and then taking these pieces and getting them together. Sometimes what he thought was gonna be one song in fact became another song, and what he thinks is the lead of this thing ends up being the end of another thing.

And this is when I started getting very close to Brian. I was coming up to the house all the time, and each time I came up he would lay a new track on us, and it was like unbelievable to hear this stuff happening. Umm, it was very hard to relate to. Without the words, just the music, it was like a symphony being written. PAUL: It still is. DAVID: Right, exactly . . . and I think then he started encountering his first problems with the Beach Boys. The first "No Brian, we shouldn't go this far out, why are we knocking success? Let's stay within the frame of, let's do the simple dumb thing, let's not go too far out, let's not lose what the Beach Boys are, uh, let's not change our physical image, let's wear the striped shirts and the white pants." The clean-cut image, which changed, if you remember, with the English recognition . . .

PAUL: Was there a ringleader on this? DAVID: Uh, no, you couldn't really say a ringleader. I think probably the most antagonistic situation was between Brian and Mike Love, although it is not an antagonistic kind of . . . They're very close, there's a great deal of love between all the fellas. I don't think any of the other boys, except perhaps for Carl, is anywhere near where Brian is musically; although Dennis showed some great moments, he was doing some of his own things and they were very beautiful . . . But Brian would come in, and he would want to do different things, and they really would balk at that; and again, I have to keep thinking that this is the problem with what's going on right now. Sooner or later it has to tire you out, and Brian would complain about it. It would be much easier for Brian to go in and lay all those voices out himself, and do all those things; there's a lot of things on *Pet Sounds* that, uh – incredible vocal things that are all Brian's voices, 'cause he can sing all their parts.

But he would go through a tremendous paranoia before he would get into the studio, knowing he was going to have to face an argument. He would come into the studio uptight, he would give a part to one of the fellas or to a group of the fellas, say, "This is what I would like to have done," and there would be resistance. And it wouldn't be happening and there would be endless takes, and then he would just junk it. And then maybe after they left to go out on tour he would come back in and do it himself. All their parts. But it was very taxing, and it was extremely painful to watch. Because it was, uh, a great wall had been put down in front of creativity.

And now, maybe, he just doesn't want to fight any more. It used to be a big fight thing in that studio, and he just may be damn well tired of fighting and having to give the parts to the guys and hearing their excuses why they don't want to do it this way or why they want to do it that way . . . that could very easily be it. Maybe he's biding his time; I don't know. I really . . . it just, uh, this is very scary. Something's gonna happen with Brian; we all know it. Those of us who've been around him know that something very quickly is gonna explode and it's gonna be beautiful, whatever it is, but I don't think it's gonna be with the Beach Boys. I would almost say for sure that the next big Brian Wilson thing will not be with the Beach Boys.

Now here's an important thing, though, which explains somewhat *Smiley Smile* and maybe *Wild Honey*: Brian, a long time ago, was incredibly interested in humor, pure, beautiful, positive humor. And if you listen to the Beatles now, and the Stones and the Airplane, and everyone else who's doing – Janis Ian, I just heard her second album, which is incredibly bad, but she has that whole number going with the wrong things and laughing and all, everyone having a good time at the session and ha ha, you get to listen in. Well, Brian was into that a long time ago; he wanted to put out the first pop humor album, and we spent days and nights running around the city tape recording different sounds and different things and getting into the most incredibly humorous things. PAUL: When? DAVID: About a year ago, just before the formation of Brother

45

Records. Hours upon hours upon hours of videotape ... a fantastic amount of time just spent on humor. At that time, I thought myself that it was a little crazy, that you had to maintain some sort of dignity, but Brian wanted out and out humor, complete and total humor, and was not allowed to do it. A lot of us ourselves would balk at Brian, let alone the Beach Boys, saying, you know, "Look, that's never gonna happen, Brian," and now we all have egg on our faces 'cause everything is humor now. And I don't know this whole game about so-and-so obviously is influenced by so-and-so, and so-and-so is influenced by ... you know, the comparison game. I don't know how deep that is or even if it does exist, but I have not – as I said earlier – I have not heard anything that is new to my ears. It's all silliness compared to what Brian really has, or had, a year ago, that is not on this latest stuff.

The thing that I would really like to get into at this point, though, is what was happening with Brian a year ago. *Pet Sounds* had been completed, "Good Vibrations" was climbing up the charts to be their first million-selling single, they had conquered England – we were getting daily phone calls from the guys, these incredible calls with stories about the three hundred photographers at EMI, in the *New Musical Express* they were the Number One group, they'd overtaken the Beatles, the first act to do that. The meetings between Brian and Lennon and McCartney, and all these things were going on. The first recognition of Brian from the critics, from the hippies, from the underworld, was starting to happen, it was all very beautiful, a very happy time. Brian then went into the studio and started *Smile*. The majority of his work was done while the guys were in England.

During this period the creative juices of Brian Wilson were at their absolute peak. We were talking about movies, television, radio, records, publications, art; all forms of communication were going to be attacked by the Brian Wilson mind. He wanted to change radio. *Again*, the FM concept that is happening now, what Tom Donahue is doing in San Francisco and LA, Brian had that whole number going a long time ago. We sat for hours and hours just thinking and talking about how lousy radio was, how obviously people, particularly kids, couldn't really be that happy to hear all this garbage coming over the air, the rapid delivery of the disc jockeys, the terrible advertisements ... Brian wanted humorous radio, he wanted everything to be positive, everything to be light and gentle, and no control, no direction, just a framework and whatever happens. The same for television. Same thing for motion pictures.

Everything Brian said, by the way, during this period of time, struck our ears, those of us who were around, as totally insane. And then he would keep it going and going, and force us to do things with him, and the second we did it, or heard it or saw it, we realized immediately that it was right. *Anything* he said was right, no matter how outlandish it seemed ... One of the really, uh, the uniquely beautiful things about Brian was that he never had one idea that I can remember that was simple. He never had one idea that made sense. Everything was new. Every single idea he would say had no foundation anywhere, except for his head.

This is how he got into, for instance, the chanting: one night we were at the studio, and Brian didn't feel like putting down a track. We were just laying around, and he said, "Come out here, everyone." So we all went out there, not one of us a professional, and he had us making animal noises, incredible noises, directing us from the control room: "Louder." "Softer." "More expansive." "Get in closer." The whole thing. We started off very conscious of what we were doing, looking at each other and very embarrassed, and then he just drove us into it, totally. We went into the studio and listened to it; he put it with music, we listened to it again and walked out knowing that once again Brian had done it.

This was a daily routine. To have your mind blown by something Brian was coming up with. Playing instruments at the dinner table, for instance. He was going to record a record where we would just all be playing different things, spoons, and he would have everyone doing a different rhythm. He would come by and say, "Dave, this is the rhythm I want you to do," and I would do some rhythm, and then he would go to the next person. He would get maybe fifteen people there, all doing different rhythms, and then he would come and sing over them . . . nonverbal things, just these chants, and they were absolutely stupendous. And a thing that right now hurts me personally is we used to fight him on this, saying, "Aw come on Brian, you know, forget it, man, pass, this is not gonna happen." And now we hear things that are like bad copies of what we were doing. I think had myself and a few other people really gotten behind him, and been on his side against who-ever he had to fight, it would have happened a year and a half ago.

So we're responsible, in a way I guess, for what's happening now. The Beach Boys have to be responsible in a way, all the doubters. Brian I think for the rest of his life's gonna have to fight doubters. He was very conscious of this; he said to me more than once, "Hey man, why do you fight me?" You know, "Why are you doing this?" Or things like, "Goddamn it, why can't I do things the way I want to, why do I always have to have resistance?" And I couldn't give him a good answer. I myself, being a painter, understand artistic freedom; yet he was so far ahead at that time that I couldn't even see where it was lead-ing. Or, let me put it this way, I always had to see where it was leading, whereas Brian never was concerned with where it was leading, only that it had to be done.

PAUL: Would it be fair to say that here's a guy, one of the few people outside of certain movie directors or whatever, who's really trying to work as an individual artist in the great creative tradition, but with media? And it necessitates working with other people, working with machines, working with all sorts of things that don't do just what you want them to do?
DAVID: I think that's it. As a painter it's generally me and the canvas. As a writer, it's you and the paper. Then you may have to fight censors, or editors, but since you're the editor

you've eliminated that. With Brian, it was him, then it was the Beach Boys, then it was the studio, the physical problems with electronics, then it was fighting, um, at Columbia for instance when after all these months one night one of the Columbia representatives showed up and saw Brian working the knobs on the control board and said, "You cannot do that. The engineers have to do that. You are not an engineer, you are not a Columbia engineer." Brian laughed at him, he thought the guy was putting him on. But the guy was serious.

This then started Brian's getting out of other people's studios – that, plus the fact that he couldn't get time when he wanted time, which could be like three in the morning, "Let's go record." Brian could work those knobs better than anyone I've ever seen, including any engineer. He would mix a lot of his things right there as they were recording, he wouldn't have to wait, he'd be adding his echo, mixing and blending right while they were performing. The whole process was Brian! If you allowed him, he could do the whole thing. As I said earlier, it is conceivable that *Pet Sounds* could have been done as well as it is right now, or perhaps even better, by just one man, Brian Wilson ... and that's a very frightening thought, an extremely frightening thought. Because you know this man's going to go into TV, you know this man's going to go into movies, and whatever else he's going to go into. He's not picking the easy way, he's not picking the personal art form, he's picking an art form that has all the restrictions of other people's involvement. There's nothing he can't learn. You tell Brian you can't do this in films because you don't understand; you can't be a director right away, you can't be a producer because you don't understand these certain elements. He laughs at you, because it's going to be a very short period of time before he knows those elements; not only will he know them academically, but he's gonna have that creative flow going on top of it, and it's gonna elevate him way past anyone else.

PAUL: When you came in at the *Beach Boys Today* time, what

did you think at that time, did it come up at all that he recorded "Bull Session with 'Big Daddy' " as the last track on that album? Did Brian ever mention what he had in mind? What he thought he was doing? DAVID: No. Brian would spend a great deal of time talking about things that he wanted to do, and he would do some of them, but he would also do a lot of things that none of us would ever know, before he got in and did 'em. I don't know how the hell anything like that would happen with Brian. You always have the feeling that he wasn't – he wasn't that aware of what he was doing. I mean, he knew in his head what he wanted to do, but he wasn't really aware in terms of society, or in terms of rules or mores, you know, how he was functioning within that realm. PAUL: Well, he was thoroughly aware of what he was doing, but he wasn't concerned with the same aspects of it as the rest of us. DAVID: That's the big thing with Brian. Is that he's very concerned with himself, but he's not concerned with the rest of us, other than the fact that he loves to entertain the rest of us. He really has a very positive feeling about people, incredibly so. An incredible amount of humor. Always looks for the humor in a human, if he can't find humor in the human being on any level, then that human being has to be, you know, pushed away, merely because he cannot function with him, he cannot function with people who have no humor.

Another thing: his humor is a particular kind of humor. Not being exposed, not being worldly, his humor is very Hawthorne, California. So *Smiley Smile* seems to a lot of us to be really corny, terribly corny, and very "in" on a Hawthorne level. The things I can't relate to on that album are things that I feel were like high school days to me, which to Brian are not necessarily high school days. PAUL: Did you grow up out here? DAVID: Oh yeah, I was born and raised here. PAUL: 'Cause another thing, it makes it difficult for the rest of the country to even know what it was like. Because Southern California is, it seems to me to be, twice as

American as any other part of America. DAVID: And the part of Southern California that Brian grew up in is so American, it's incredible. There's . . . I lived in a place called Inglewood, California, which is very close to Hawthorne, and what you have there is the people who came in in the thirties from Oklahoma, from the dust bowl days, and then you have a lot of people coming during the Second World War, because all the defence plants were out there. You had people coming from the Midwest to work in defence plants. So you have a tremendous amount of Midwestern culture, right there by the beach. It's kind of like Iowa with a beach, is really what it's like down there.

PAUL: It's letting go. The whole Iowa thing comes in, but loosens its belt, relaxes, so you have sort of a cross between the Midwest and the Deep South. DAVID: Yeah, there's a lot of southern influence. The one thing you don't have, is you don't have a lot of New England sophistication. Or the kind of provincial thing you get on the opposite hand in New England. You don't have any of that out here. It's really . . . and then the weather, everything in Southern California really ties in, the kind of clothes we wear, running around ten months out of the year, eleven months out of the year in the sun, a healthy physical thing. Again, another incredibly important aspect of Brian Wilson is physical health. Incredible. I could go on for hours on physical numbers we would have to go through. Brian thought we could never get anything done until we were physically able to move – then would come the head, the head would start to clear up along with the body. The swimming pool for instance with Brian was *never* thought to be a luxury. Swimming was important for physical tuning. We had a lot of business discussions right out there in the middle of the pool, because of the water gently, you know, what the water does to the body and the head. A lot of our problems were solved right out there in the pool at four o'clock in the morning when it was 28 degrees outside, standing right out there, naked as jaybirds, 92 degrees, the steam

51

flowing up, discussing heavy business. And it worked, every time.

PAUL: Is Brian very sensitive about being referred to, as he often is, in the press, as fat? DAVID: Oh, he's got to be. Oh sure. PAUL: Is he fat, really? DAVID: I don't think he is. I know he's strong as an ox. He's a fantastic athlete, very proud of the fact that he's a great athlete, good baseball player, football player, basketball, whatever. If you remember, in looking at the pictures of the Beach Boys on their first couple of albums, Brian was always very tall and skinny. Not even was he well built, but he was very thin. So it's got to hurt him. And I don't understand why people call him fat; that really is not important, except that he needs that, he needs the energy that that kind of weight puts on, to carry his mind. His mind is always working so fast and so much that if he didn't have that bulk, he wouldn't make it.

PAUL: Well, why people do it is that they're creating this whole Southern California, Beach Boy myth . . . DAVID: I guess the same way they talk about Dennis's muscles, 'cause he's so muscular. PAUL: And it's something that tends to offend people, you know, when the group comes on stage. People are most of all offended by the Beach Boys on stage, or were . . . DAVID: By chubby little Carl, and – PAUL: And the way Mike Love carried on, and then everything just seemed to . . . DAVID: And the clothes, the striped shirts and the white buck shoes, and the slacks and the whole thing. They're not like that offstage, that was the great paradox, is that they in their own ways were as hip as anyone I've ever met. I know that they always used to talk about Brian wearing striped shirts, the striped surfer shirts offstage and the white pants and all, that's groovy, I mean what does that have to do with the whole number? Other than the fact that yes he is presenting himself, he is what he is and he's presenting himself physically. I guess if he wore a cape they'd be a lot happier.

II

PAUL: Let's try to take it historically... some of the development of *Pet Sounds* we got into, some we didn't. You know, starting from "Sloop John B," what came, what got built, to the point that it finally became a whole album, and what he started out thinking of the album as, what he ended up thinking of it as, and then the transition from that into *Smile*... DAVID: Well, the first thing Brian will come up with is a concept, an album concept; generally he wants to do a thing. I say "a thing" because it's, you don't really know what it is, he throws out a whole bunch of words at you, one-liners, and words and half-phrases, and you really don't know what he's talking about at all. All you know is to go along with it. The Beach Boys could walk into a session and not have the slightest idea what they're recording that night. He tells them what to record, and they do it. They don't know what it means, generally, and that was always a problem too. We're gonna do a piece of this, and a piece of that, a fragment, and they would do it, as instruments.

So with *Pet Sounds*, *Pet Sounds* to my knowledge was never *Pet Sounds* until the end, it was just things he was recording. He would get a musical idea. He would then extend off that musical idea. In doing that extension, something else would pop up. So he would stop the first thing and then take off on the second thing. He would develop the new concept that hit his head, until he came to another concept. He would then abandon for a while that second thing and start off on the third, so that what he was doing was building, like with blocks or a web; that's why there was the beautiful consistency within *Pet Sounds*, musically. His things tie together so tight because, as I said earlier, what is at one time the first song, may later be part of the sixth.

And then the lyrics started happening, at the same time. He may get into a feeling on one thing. He'll play, he'll hear a track, and he'll say gee this track is a beautiful thing to express a feeling between a guy and a girl, or this one should be a relationship between this and this. Then he'll start to do the words on it. Then it becomes a song, and then it gets a title, the titles really don't mean anything, I sometimes don't think the words mean anything in certain places. But that's how he builds an album, that's how *Pet Sounds* came about.

PAUL: Did the beginnings of work on *Pet Sounds* coincide with his decision to stop traveling with the group? DAVID: Definitely. It was also the beginning of his sound effects, which in a way was the beginning of sound effects in pop music, on the level that it is now. *Pet Sounds* is directly related to the last little track with the train and the two dogs, the two dogs are his dogs, they are family to him. He was very happy with *Pet Sounds*. Extremely happy with that album, thought that he had done something very important, and was very unhappy that it didn't do well commercially, for the first time he was aware of that.

But he'd experimented, and succeeded. So therefore when it was time to get into *Smile*, the initial involvement into *Smile*, it was just impossible to keep up with that man. He was setting up blocks of studio time, would get uptight if he couldn't get a studio at four, four in the morning. He'd be sitting around and he'd get an idea, and he'd want to be able to go in the next morning, like at seven or eight, and record. Couldn't do that, obviously, because you can't operate that way. Again, one of the restrictions . . . But his whole attitude towards *Smile* was another extension of *Pet Sounds*. Certain things had happened in *Pet Sounds* for him, for the first time, and he really wanted to get that in *Smile*. It was going to be a monument. That's the way we talked about it, as a monument.

Brian got in with Van Dyke Parks at this time. PAUL: How did that happen? DAVID: I'm not sure really how that happened. My involvement with Brian when Van Dyke entered the picture was still on a very social level. I remember one night talking to someone, and someone said, "Van Dyke has been up to Brian's house and they're gonna work together." And I thought, "Wow! Man, that's gonna be unbelievable!" And I was perplexed as to how the two of them came together. PAUL: Was Michael Vosse in the picture at this time? DAVID: Michael was just starting to get into the picture. Paul Robbins was starting to get into the picture at this time. Then when I started coming up to the house a whole bunch, when the Brother Records thing started to happen, Van was there like all the time. And Van and Brian were running together, very hot and heavy. And Van was blowing Brian's mind, and Brian was blowing Van's mind. And I looked at the whole situation and I said, at that time, "That's never going to work. Those two are never gonna be able to work together."

And they never have, they never really did. They had a great moment of creativity. I think Van Dyke is one of the very few people that Brian truly looked at on an equal level. Or maybe that's a little presumptuous to say. Van Dyke blew Brian's mind and I hadn't seen anyone else do that. And Van used to walk away, from his evenings with Brian, very awestruck at what Brian was doing musically. I think to this day Van Dyke is the first one to admit – again, not the influence but the effect that Brian had, or has, on Van Dyke. Very strong. Their parting was kind of tragic, in the fact that there were two people who absolutely did not want to separate but they both knew that they had to separate, that they could not work together. 'Cause they were too strong, you know, in their own areas. PAUL: When, February? DAVID: Right around February, yeah. Van was getting – his lyric was too sophisticated, and in some areas Brian's music was not sophisticated enough, and so they started clashing on that. PAUL: They missed each other. DAVID: Yeah. They were together to a certain point, and then zingo! they bypassed each other, and never the twain shall meet with those two.

PAUL: Let's try to remember the tracks. "The Elements" . . . DAVID: Okay. *Smile* was going to be the culmination of all of Brian's intellectual preoccupations; and he was really into the elements. He ran up to Big Sur for a week, just 'cause he wanted to get into that, up to the mountains, into the snow, down to the beach, out to the pool, out at night, running around, to water fountains, to a lot of water, the sky, the whole thing was this fantastic amount of awareness of his surroundings. So the obvious thing was to do something that would cover the physical surroundings.

We were aware, he made us aware, of what fire was going to be, and what water was going to be; we had some idea of air. That was where it stopped. None of us had any ideas as to how it was going to tie together, except that it appeared to us to be an opera. And the story of the fire part I guess is pretty well known by now. PAUL: There's a lot of confusion about it. DAVID: Well, briefly, Brian created a track for the fire part which was the most revolutionary sound I've ever heard. He actually created a fire, a forest fire, with instruments, no sound effects – a lot of strings, and a lot of technique on the board – when you would listen to that thing it would actually, it would scare you, you would be scared listening to that. It was so overpowering . . . and then there was a rash of fires in the city, and Brian became very aware of this rash of fires, and then there was the fire across the street from the studio . . . Brian's not superstitious, he's something that I can't name, 'cause I totally do not understand what it is, but he had a series of dialogues with me where at one point he asked if I would check the fire department, call the city fire department or whoever it was that I would have to call, to find out if there were more fires within this period in Los Angeles than in any other period in history. Because he really felt, I guess the word is vibrations. Brian is very into vibrations, and made me, to this day, very aware of vibrations. Anyway, after we all laughed at him, as we normally did in these situations, he went ahead and destroyed the tape. Completely. Eliminated it, never to be heard again. That basically destroyed "Elements."

PAUL: Was this the first break in *Smile*, the first turn downward? DAVID: Yeah. That was the first sign that we were going to have problems on this album. That, and the fact that for the first time Brian was having trouble with studios – getting studio time. Then he was having a problem with engineers. Brian was starting to meet a fantastic amount of resistance on all fronts. Like, very slowly everything started to collapse about him. The scene with Van Dyke. Now, that's a critical point. You've gotta remember that originally Van Dyke was gonna do all the lyrics for S*mile*. Then there was a hassle between Van and Brian and Van wasn't around. So that meant that Brian was now going to have to finish some of the lyrics himself. Well, how was he gonna put his lyrics in with the lyrics already started by Van Dyke? So he stopped recording for a while. Got completely away from music, saying, it's time to get into films. And we all knew what was happening.

So he abandoned the studio. Then, there was the business, Brother Records. He got his head into the business aspects of Brother Records. So that kept him out of . . . he had another excuse. Then there was the attention. David Oppenheim coming into town to do the Leonard Bernstein special on pop, and there was that whole number going on. And this guy coming up from that paper, and you yourself came up, and a lot of people started coming, people that Brian had never met before, *kinds* of people that Brian had never met before. So he was spending a lot of his time questioning me as to the validity of critics, the importance of certain people, why is it important that all of a sudden they're doing this, and all the time knowing that it was important, but not being able, because he'd not been exposed in the past, not being able to tell who was real and who was not real. There was gonna be the *Post* article by Jules Siegel, he was on television, an incredible amount of excuses not to cut, things to get into. The little film for "Good Vibrations," which took time away; the guys being out of town, whatever, he was clinging onto excuses.

And I was very aware of what was happening, but I couldn't put my finger onto why *Smile* was now starting to nose-dive, other than the fact that I still felt at that point that the central thing was Van Dyke's severing of that relationship. PAUL: The creative period had been passed and the specific concept was beginning to slip away. DAVID: Right. What had happened was, Brian had gone in and had done a fantastic amount of recording while the guys were in Europe, and then there was a separation of time, and then it got to be, well, as soon as they get back we'll finish. And they got back. And they had their normal rest time. And then he brought them into the studio, and they were hearing things they never heard before. Not only were they hearing things they'd never heard from Brian, but you've got to remember that none of this [1967] Beatles stuff was happening then. There was no way to relate to what Brian was putting down.

That's when he started meeting resistance from the Beach Boys. "Brian, what are you . . . what is this? What are you doing? This is not within our framework, you're going too far now Brian, this is too experimental. I can't sing this part." In one specific song Brian wanted to sing the lead, but it was almost promised to Mike. And Mike couldn't cut it the way Brian wanted it to be cut, although Mike was cutting it beautifully. But it still wasn't right, and Brian wanted to do it . . . they went through an incredible amount of time, almost a whole week of wasted studio time, before Brian finally did it.

Brian didn't know how to deal with the boys. We were around for the first time; the Beach Boys came back from England and here was this bunch of people, who all of a sudden were saying a lot of things – Michael Vosse, and myself, and Paul Robbins somewhat, Van Dyke, very strongly, Jules, a lot of people they hadn't seen before and that must have been very scary for them, 'cause here was a whole bunch of people who were doing heavy things for their career, their future. And here's Brian, with entirely new sounds. I think had they relaxed into *Smile, Smile* would have happened. 'Cause you've got to remember, to this day *Smile* is still an album of tracks that are filed away somewhere, not many vocals down, but there's still a whole album – there's enough there for three albums of incredible tracks.

"Heroes and Villains" was a critical track on the album. Would have been a critical part of *Smile* in its original form, not in the form that came out. Now here's another thing that happened. Now he's involved with the lawyers. Now he's involved with Capitol Records, and we're into a lawsuit, we're into a very big lawsuit . . . How do we get into a lawsuit and still maintain our positive image? We cannot be the villains, remember; we've got to be the heroes, at all times. We cannot be bad guys. All right Brian, he was told one day, at this point in order for us to get what we have to get for Brother Records, we've got to have a single out. That old, lousy thing that still exists in our business: you've got to have the single out. There's always a reason. Whether it's for the lawsuit, or because your image is failing, or you haven't had one out in five months, or the last one trailed off, or the last one was a million-seller, whatever, there's always that lousy you've-got-to-have-your-single.

So Brian is told that he's got to have a single. I told Brian he had to have a single. It was the hardest thing I ever did. Brian was not at those meetings with the Capitol people. I was there. And I was in the meetings with the lawyers. Brian was not there. Nick Grillo and I would have to go to these situations, and then relate them back to Brian. It was very difficult for me to do, because I was on Brian's side. Yet, he wanted Brother Records, and I had to do the Brother Records thing and that really started to kill the creativity that was happening in *Smile*. He was getting very up tight, he was getting disappointed, he was getting disappointed in me, because now I was being business and I wasn't being, you know, I wasn't hanging out with Brian at night any more, because I had to be in an office in the morning, there was none of the five o'clock in the morning sillinesses that we used to go through. There was now calling up Brian, instead of saying let's hang out, it was Hey Brian you've got to give me an answer to something blah blah blah blah you know business, business. All this was in the framework of the fact that a normal business meeting with

Brian Wilson usually meant going up to Brian's about one in the morning, going into the tent, getting it on, getting out our pieces of paper and pencils, and sitting there, and he would say okay, now: here's the structure for the business. And it would be: Number one, health. Number two, foods. Then we'd list a, b, and c, health foods. Number three, swimming. Charts. Maps. He wanted anatomy charts all over the place. Awareness of surroundings, awareness of health and all of this.

All of a sudden that was gone. Now it was, uh, Brian, we can go for half a million dollars, we can go for a million dollars blah blah. And all this was happening to him. He had to get out of the creative thing. It was just an absolute must. So that when I left, "Heroes and Villains" was being planned to be a single, only because it was the closest thing to being finished, at that point, and sadly not even the original "Heroes and Villains" because right at that time *Sergeant Pepper* came out. PAUL: When I was there in December, Brian was thinking of "Heroes and Villains" as the single. DAVID: Right. He would think of "Heroes and Villains," and then he would call up two nights later and say it was going to be this, and it was going to be that, and it was going to be "Heroes and Villains" again, and then everyone said, No, Brian, it should be "Heroes and Villains," no Brian it should be this . . . See, people should never be allowed to say "No" to Brian Wilson. Brian is a person that never should be said no to. 'Cause if you just get behind him, or next to him, and go with him, it's gonna come out okay.

But he was forced into that. And maybe that's why what's happening now is happening. He probably hasn't recovered from that. It was a big shock for him. It's like taking a person, exposing him to something he's always wanted to be in, taking him right to the brink of it, and leaving. And saying, "Geez Brian, how come you haven't followed up with that whole thing? Why have you fallen down?" He zoomed right up there, alienated from a lot of things that had been his strengths in the past. Those strengths were ripped away, shown to be shallow and phony, taken away from him . . . but no foundation

60

put under him. And the foundation that we all had, that we were trying to supply him with, was us! And when we went, there was nothing left there. Just him, hanging . . . and, um, perhaps we should have never gone in the first place. I don't know what his development would've been; I don't think he would've gotten into some of those things on *Smile*, though, had he not been exposed to this whole new thing . . .

And he's gonna recover. But *Smile* . . . I don't know, I don't even know how many tracks he finished, or worked on: there's "The Elements," "Heroes and Villains," um . . . "Surf's Up," which is a masterpiece, unbelievable . . . That was the one song, "Surf's Up" was the one perfect blending of Van Dyke and Brian. Absolute perfection. One of the most important songs I've ever heard in my life. I don't know if it will ever be out. Let's see, what else is there . . . PAUL: "The Child Is the Father of the Man." DAVID: Which I understand will be on his next album. I just heard that from someone, I don't remember who told me . . . A couple of Indian things, "Bicycle Rider." PAUL: Wasn't that part of "Heroes and Vil-lains"? DAVID: At one time. It was also part of something else. Um . . . "Vegetables." PAUL: How was that going to be? DAVID: Not like it is on the album. It's on *Smiley Smile*, it was changed quite a bit. See, all that stuff was changed, because Brian . . . none of the tracks are on *Smiley Smile*. Some of the songs are there, but he's recorded them in the house. "Heroes and Villains," yes, some of the tracks were from the original. Ah . . . he was forced to put "Good Vibrations" on, something he never wanted to do is put a single onto the album, but he was forced to do that. For sales. That was another, I'm sure, a minor tragedy for him.

I think what Brian tried to do with *Smiley Smile* is he tried to salvage as much of *Smile* as he could and at the same time immediately go into his humor album. 'Cause it's so – I hear elements in that of our discussions about the humor album, just little pieces of it. PAUL: "Little Pad" is really nice. DAVID: Yeah. Right. But you can see that there's a man straining when he makes that album; you can see that there's a man not caring when you hear *Wild Honey*. PAUL: Yeah. "Heroes and Villains" is beautiful the way it came out, in a certain sense . . . the point where it turns upside down, from animate to inanimate, from the voices to the organ . . . but the mix isn't quite as it should be, it sounds harsh to the ear . . . DAVID: That's another thing that is a key indication, is that Brian's mixing on the last two albums is nowhere near what it was on *Pet Sounds* . . . you can tell on *Pet Sounds* there's a man who really cared a lot about mixing, as he did on a lot of his other things. You don't get that feeling any more.

I don't know what the relationship between Brian and the Boys is at this point, 'cause I haven't been around, but that's gotta be affected, that's gotta be a cause of what we're hearing now. During *Pet Sounds* it was at a very good point. It was never really at a good point during *Smile*. A lot of problems, a lot of internal problems, again, because of Brother Records, because of the newness of what he was doing, their new position in the music world. Derek was around at that time . . .

PAUL: I'd like to talk about Derek. DAVID: Okay; one of my favorite all-time people. Derek Taylor I think is singly responsible for what happened in England, if nothing more than by exposing them, to England, to the right people, getting them and the Beatles together, and then getting that into the proper papers, that they were getting together. Coordinating the people who were getting to Brian. The English thing was Derek's. Derek's relationship with Brian was at first very strong, then went through a tremendous nose dive; they both decided to sever relationships, then they came back again, and they worked well for a while, got along very well with the other boys, and then it nosed off again, into another direction.

Brian always felt that the Beach Boys were always number two with Derek, the Beatles were always number one. He had a very strong feeling about that. And uh . . . it's a silly thing I think in a way, but at the same time totally understandable. Belonging to a record label, you see that with your own artists on the label, when one act is hot the other ones always get that paranoia, "you care more about them," you know, and it's very silly but at the same time it's an ego thing and ego things do exist, and you can't fight 'em. PAUL: That's true, and it comes from fear. DAVID: Right. But Derek did a magnificent job with the Beach Boys, I mean he did a superb job . . . they were known at that time as the faceless monsters, and he made personalities out of them.

PAUL: We talked a little about Brian's view of the world and an obvious thematic thing that we've been into is the relationship between him and the rest of the world, mostly in layers – the immediate people around him, the business world, the music business, a little further out the audience . . . The basic problem we're faced with is a great concept and a man who is capable of actually administrating that concept, and yet it did not happen. DAVID: I think the easiest way to get into this is to understand first of all that Brian is tremendously compulsive on all levels . . . and the compulsive pattern is most apparent in his relationship to individuals. You can always tell how effective a relationship is in the fact that Brian will try to show you he's ignoring something that has happened. If somebody says something that you know has hurt Brian, his immediate reaction will be to slough it off, it doesn't bother me. And you really think that it doesn't bother him, but then you'll notice that for three days he hasn't been in the studio, or for two days he hasn't smiled – you'll start noticing there are certain things about him that aren't happening. If he were having trouble with a musical idea in his head, and he got in a fight with Marilyn, the two of 'em would, it would be like a volcano. It was always that his problems with his music were one part of a combustible formula for an explosion, and anything that would happen around that would be the oxygen, let's say, and his was the fuel, and it would explode. And it would generally explode in the manner that he would become useless in terms of musical effectiveness, he would be totally useless for a great period of time.

Brian cannot go into a session with something happening in the back of his head and put that back there and hold it there and do his work. His life is his work and if he has an argument with his father at twelve o'clock in the afternoon, and it's sufficient enough argument to cause him to worry or to grieve, he's not going to be able to cut at twelve o'clock midnight. He's not going to be able to do anything effective on an artistic level until he gets that problem resolved in his head or his heart, wherever it has struck him. And the same thing with the boys, with the brothers and Mike Love, or strangers, me, Michael Vosse, whoever. Whoever would come around . . . a writer, would come up, say something wrong, strike him wrong; he'd be upset for a couple of days. Those two days were lost. He would try, he would try almost heroically to get something done, but he couldn't. It would just be like terror, it would be a lot of wasted time running around doing this, running around doing that, let's start working on the comedy album, let's go out and record water fountains, let's go out and, for instance, one night he wanted us to go into a bar and start a fight. So he could record it. And that's really carrying something pretty far.

PAUL: That's a really good example of what I was just thinking, namely that here you have a man, a really brilliant man, so that, theoretically, whatever it takes to get whatever he wants to do done is worthwhile. But to what extent is it humanly possible, for however many people it takes, to completely, for an extended period of time, go on another person's trip, and be off or just not functioning when he can't function, and be ready to go the minute – seven o'clock in the morning in the studio, whatever – that he wants to . . . to what extent is it necessary, to what extent is it possible for the people around somebody like Brian to do this? DAVID: That's one of the best questions I've ever been asked in terms of Brian Wilson, 'cause that is the heart of a relationship with Brian. To answer one part of that question, it is absolutely necessary, if you're related on any level with Brian Wilson, to be in that position, to be

64

ready at a moment's call to get out of bed and go up to the house and rap, not because he's doing it on an ego level, not because he wants to know that he's king in your part of the court, but because he needs it. And he can't find it with anyone except you at that moment.

Now, on the other hand, who can do that? Certainly I couldn't, 'cause I'm not there any more; Michael Vosse couldn't, 'cause he's not there any more, all those people couldn't, 'cause none of 'em are around any more. It's impossible – unless you have the metabolism of Brian Wilson, you can't stay on his trip. And to be related with Brian Wilson is to be on Brian Wilson's trip. You will never be with Brian Wilson on your trip, you'll always be on his trip. Because he's an artist, and he demands that. And if you don't want to be on his trip, then you pass. We all have our little things, I guess; we all have people around who travel on our trips individually; his trip is just a fantasy, that's the whole beauty of Brian's trip, is that it's an absolute fantasy, it's like living Disneyland. There's no way to relate to it at all. PAUL: True creativity . . . the ability to make something up out of nothing. DAVID: Continually! And each thing more fantastic than the one previous! PAUL: Steady state theory of the universe. DAVID: Right.

There is one fellow who is around, who's been around for a long time with Brian, who has been able to stay on his trip, a kid named Arnie Geller, who should never be taken lightly. Arnie is Boswell to Brian's Johnson. He's a very important person in Brian's life; he is the person who will always be there. And because of that, he allows Brian to get things done. If there's no one around, when Brian needs someone, I don't think Brian can get that much done. Except writing. He needs no one for his music. Just him for his music. But to function as a human, he needs company, he needs people. Arnie . . . Arnie is the one who designed the cover for *Wild Honey*, he is basically an artist. His function is as an artist, graphic artist; I imagine he, at this point, is also Brian's contact with the office, with Brother Records, with Nick Grillo, who runs the office for the Beach Boys, he runs all their functions for them . . . Uh, I don't like to say Arnie is Brian's man, because that's like degrading him, and he shouldn't be degraded. He's his partner. He's his comrade. He's his friend.

Another one who's close is Steve Korthof, who is a relative of the Beach Boys; businesswise, he's, for lack of a better word, a band boy, but he's not their band boy, he's more than that. Again, he's a friend. He's a confidant. He is a solid foundation in their whole thing. He's one of the most beautiful people I've ever known. And very important in the Beach Boys picture, very important in Brian Wilson's picture. He travels with the guys, on the road. Takes care of the equipment. Watches the sound. Takes care of their personal problems. But not in terms of, "Hey, Steve, run down and get me a Coke." He's not a go-for. Dennis is having problems, Steve goes to Dennis's room and raps with him, gets him out of his problem. One of the guys doesn't want to do something, Steve is the one who's sent. Then when he's in town, he always happens to find his way up to Brian's house at very critical moments. He's foundation. He's physically strong, morally strong, and something that Brian can always relate to; one of the few people Brian can always relate to in any dangerous situation. He knows he can always get Steve, and Steve will get it done. Steve will take care of the situation. And when you're as volatile as Brian Wilson is, you need that. Without Steve and Arnie I think Brian wouldn't even be able to do the albums he's doing now. He'd be totally ineffectual, in terms of moving around in the outside world.

. . . Marilyn, is a saint! Marilyn is unbelievable. Marilyn is the perfect artist's wife, or lover, or mate; she's everything. She puts up – obviously – with the most incredible, impossible scenes I have ever been involved in; she puts up with a man who at one time is a raving lunatic, at another moment, an absolute saint. You know, that tremendous paradox of personalities. They fight, and they love. She's always there. There's a great feeling I get from being close to both of them, there's a great feeling of love.

That's his tangible man-woman love, Marilyn. She can be the mistress of the home, 'cause Brian likes to entertain; but Brian does not entertain like anyone I've ever seen entertain. Brian can have a dinner, which he did lots of times, a dinner for a lot of people, which for two days ahead of time he's incredibly excited about; gets the people up to the house that he wants up to the house; and then won't show for dinner. In the middle of dinner he'll run in maybe and wolf down the food in three seconds and he's gone again. She keeps that whole thing together. When Brian gets into his very deep depressions, Marilyn is the only one I've ever seen able to really get to him. She's a very beautiful person; very simple, very plain, exactly what he needs. Very, very groovy.

PAUL: Is there a song that's, particularly – DAVID: For her? I couldn't say. I don't know. See, you never know with him, he doesn't give you those clues. Brian doesn't make his work obvious, like a lot of writers. Brian is absolutely unpretentious as an artist. He just is not aware of creating things, images and symbols and creating a life and taking advantage of the position he's in. So you never know with Brian, he just goes, he just does his thing. And you really never know exactly what that thing is.

There's a strong mother and father thing happening with Brian; sometimes it's very negative, sometimes it's very positive. Extreme in both cases. I mean, it's not a normal son/parent relationship, it's a very active relationship between family. Extremely close to the mother, and very tight bond between father and son. Also a competition between father and son, that sometimes gets very sticky. I don't think fathers and sons should be in competition . . . A factor that affects Brian's creativity. A bad note from the father or a bad scene with the father can affect Brian for weeks, days; in the same way, a good thing with his father can put him in a state of exhilaration. Exaltation. So it's very critical at that point.

. . . Dennis. Dennis is the kind of person that will ask you to go shopping with him, and whatever he buys for himself he'll buy for you. That's Dennis. He will go out to get a motor-cycle, and if you're with him, he'll buy you a motorcycle. Incredibly . . . always on edge, completely on edge, you never know with Dennis at any second whether he's gonna explode or not. No matter whether he's happy or sad. He is completely free, an animal, a free animal who is almost always controlled by his emotions, and very seldom by his head. A beautiful younger brother, and one that Brian can relate to – a very easy brother relationship for Brian to relate to and also a source of incredible enjoyment for Brian. Brian would spend a great deal of time talking about Dennis, just going into big raps about Dennis. Apparently the easiest one of all for Brian to understand. He still has a physical thing that Brian can relate to, the strength, the athletic ability, the whole thing. PAUL: Surfing came from Dennis. DAVID: Right. Hot rods. PAUL: The enthusiasm. DAVID: Dennis. Always Dennis. Even the love of outdoors. But here's the interesting thing. All the fantasies Brian would get, Dennis would take even farther. In other words, Brian would come up with the ideas, but once he would lay them on Dennis's head, they were gone. I mean, Dennis would shoot 'em right to the extreme. Brian would say it would really be groovy if everyone got into the ocean, Dennis would buy a boat. Brian would still talk about the ocean, or he'd rent a boat and go out. If Brian said, "God, it would be great to have motorcycles," Dennis would have a motorcycle outfit, a motorcycle, and would be doing the most incredible mountain-climbing numbers you've ever seen. That's Dennis.

And Carl is the spirit. Brian goes to Carl for the spiritual thing. Brian feels that Carl is the most spiritual person he's ever personally known. And perhaps he is; I don't know. There's a certain something . . . the vibration thing is Carl. Brian is deeply, emotionally involved with Carl. On a very, very heavy level. PAUL: Is Carl the youngest brother? DAVID: Yeah. PAUL: Are there only the three? DAVID: Yeah, there's the three brothers and then Mike Love, who's a cousin. PAUL: Is there a sister? DAVID: No. That's the family.

PAUL: What does the brother thing have to do with the group? DAVID: The brother thing is obviously very strong, in the fact that Brian is still producing the Beach Boys, when as I said earlier it would be much easier for him to produce himself. That's the Beach Boys. They're always my brothers and then the Beach Boys. Always my brothers first. The whole Beach Boy mystique, the Beach Boy thing, the thing that I used to get a great deal of personal fun out of, is when people would arbitrarily slough off or slam the Beach Boys as being wimp, or whatever they wanted to call 'em, they really had no idea of the incredible complex thing that is happening amongst a group of people. You could do a trilogy just on the lives of the Beach Boys. There is so much emotion, and drama, in that family, much more than I've ever seen in any other family, and everything directly affects Brian. Brian is always conscious of those boys, continually conscious of them, as brothers and as human beings. Very seldom as an act.

Again, that's why, a great reason why *Smile* wasn't finished, the way Brian wanted it, because of their resistance in the studio. PAUL: And one way of finishing it would have been to break up the group. But he didn't do that. DAVID: Which he talked about. On many occasions. But it was easier, I think, to get rid of the outsiders like myself than it was to break up the brothers. You can't break up brothers.

. . . Mike Love? Businessman. Continually being accused by Brian of being mercenary, soulless – very untrue, Mike is a very soulful person. He's the only one really who is aware of business, for the group. At the same time Michael is the one who has opposed experimentation stronger than anyone else. He's the one more divorced of the family relationship in the group. Brian's opposite number, you know, he's the one who is continually fighting Brian, the hardest one for Brian to control, the hardest one for Brian to deal with; and I've seen Mike send Brian right out of sessions, because Brian will get so frustrated in terms of trying to relate to Mike, and not being able to. Brian will just stomp right out, and there's some more lost time, more lost creative time. Mike was the easiest one for me to relate to, outside of Brian. I had a very simple time with Mike, because Mike understood what I was trying to do on a business level.

PAUL: When *Wild Honey* does not make the top fifty albums [blush. It did. It made it to thirty], will this bring some kind of realization down on their heads? DAVID: They realize it now, they realize it *right* now. They realized it when "Heroes and Villains" didn't get higher than it did, coming off of "Good Vibrations." They realized it when *Smiley Smile* bombed. They realize it now that "Wild Honey," the single, has never been played on the radio in LA, where they're born, where they're from . . . PAUL: What do they realize? That Brian has to be set free? Or just that . . . DAVID: That something is wrong.

Brian knows, I'm sure Brian knows what's wrong. PAUL: He might even be afraid, of what it really is, because it's an ego trip, eventually, and we're all afraid of ego trips. DAVID: I think Brian is probably saying to himself a little bit, "I should have taken the other course. I should have gone ahead the way I was going to go ahead and abandoned the Beach Boys." He's gotta be thinking of that sometimes. Because he was peaking, at one point, and then it came down. They may be thinking that he is experimenting, although listening to *Wild Honey* there's certainly no experimentation on that album, at all.

I mean, how could a group drop as quickly as they've dropped, when they've been around so long? This isn't Question Mark & the Mysterians. PAUL: It's a time problem, there's a time problem: I'll tell you the answer to that one, because you're too close to it to see. They've only had two singles in the top ten in the last two years. Think about that. Two years! There is a turnover in the rock and roll audience of more than 50 percent in two years. And the people they've alienated have been their old-time audience, and they haven't picked up their new audience yet . . . DAVID: Well, you're right. The problem . . . you're right, though, the problem is they alienated their old-time audience with *Pet Sounds*. *Pet Sounds* was the first Beach

Boy album not to be a million-seller, not to zoom right up there. They lost the teenyboppers, but they gained the other, you know, the underground, or whatever tag you want to put . . . PAUL: They *started* to, they only barely started to. DAVID: They got us, they put hooks in us . . . PAUL: Yeah, but still you run into more people than you can believe who just don't know about the Beach Boys, who should. DAVID: Well, the thing I was going to say was the ones that they hooked, they immediately lost, with the release of "Heroes and Villains," then with the album. PAUL: *Smiley Smile* was good, but it was a disappointment.

DAVID: Mmm. They're in desperate trouble right now, and it's got to be affecting Brian, and the sad thing is, for me personally, and this is why I'm very happy to be talking to you, is all those I-told-you-so's are able to say I told you so at this point, the San Francisco crowd, who called the Beach Boys at one time the California Hypes. Umm . . . All the other people who have said, "What a hype job that is," and my concern at this point is that Brian does what I know he has, you know, does his thing. PAUL: That he pull it back together. DAVID: It's there, it's there, and he's the giant, he really is the giant. And if something doesn't happen soon, he may completely abandon the whole situation.

6

Mass Consumption of the World

David Anderle and I had only met once or twice before the afternoon we recorded parts I and II of this conversation. Months later, at the beginning of March 1968, we got together again, this time at David's home in Silverlake if I'm remembering right.

III

[Three months have passed since the first segments of this discussion were recorded.] DAVID: I really didn't get into the *Wild Honey* album until *John Wesley Harding* came out and everybody started saying, "Dylan has told 'em what to do, he's leading the way again, he's told everyone to go back to simplicity and forget wild production albums and just put it right where it's at." And all of a sudden I realized that once again Brian had been first.

That's exactly what *Wild Honey* is, man, that's just what it is. It's getting right back to simplicity and right back to music. And forget about how weird you can get, on an album. To me, anyway . . . that's exactly what it says to me. That, plus the fact that it's really Brian doing what he's always wanted to do. I remember when he first wrote "Surf's Up" and everybody was so excited when it was just him and the piano, and it was at that point that you could . . . if you were around at that time, you really understood where Brian's musical head was at. That same kind of need, and pleading, and his incredible loneliness

73

were all expressed in *Wild Honey*, that kind of soul singing that he's doing. So yeah, *Wild Honey* is very groovy.

PAUL: I think the . . . the step that's been made by a number of people recently – Dylan, Brian, whoever – is not exactly a step towards simplicity – maybe some kind of artistic consciousness – the thing is, it has to include the Love album [*Forever Changes*], and the Byrds album [*The Notorious Byrd Brothers*], which are obviously the same thing but which aren't "simple," on that level. DAVID: No, well, when I speak of simplicity I'm thinking in terms of what we are always told is the true art form, which is simplicity. It's not necessarily something that is simple, as such, or dumb, those are not the things that I think of . . . it's an elimination of all those things that are not necessary to make your statement. Or, um, synthesizing everything. PAUL: Yeah, making it into a unity, a monolith. DAVID: Exactly, and that's what *Wild Honey* is.

I still have to think about *Smile* a lot, that stuff that you and I heard was very complex, on many levels. But Brian was never, Brian is never complex in terms of his music – he's a complex personality, of course, but he's . . . Everything with Brian is direct and forceful and the quickest way it can get said, and again, this is *Wild Honey*. It is to me. I remember so many things that went on when I was around Brian, now when I listen to *Wild Honey*, so many things that he said, so many things that he did, and now I'm really anxious to hear the next one. I'm *really* anxious to hear his next album.

PAUL: What I feel about *Wild Honey*, and our reaction to it, is that rock had been building up to a peak of achievement on a certain level, we'd gone about as far as we could go from a given premise, which means *Wild Honey* and the Dylan album and all can be seen as some sort of breakthrough. And when that happens, whenever we emerge newborn on a higher level and we have to be small all over again, and beginning to grow – well, we get confused, we get uncertain; for a moment we feel that this new stuff has no merit at all – and it doesn't, by the old standards. 'Cause we're in a whole new place, we're dealing in new basics instead of the incredible complexities that had grown out of the old basics. The transition from *Sergeant Pepper* to *Wild Honey* is kind of like the New Year's Eve cartoons of the old man and the baby . . .

DAVID: Yeah. I think the first indication of how absurd the musical thing was getting, in terms of what we're talking about now, was "A Day in the Life." When Lennon would get into the instrumental thing, that fantastic driving until all of a sudden you realize that this is a piece of plastic or this is a piece of music and you can't explode out and disappear, no matter how many instruments you put on something, no matter what you do with the board. And I think then "I Am the Walrus" was another extreme case, to me that was extreme absurdity – and where do you go from there, and why do you have to go there? Except as a trip maybe . . . But that's not the answer, I think Brian knows that, and I think Dylan knows that . . . If "Lady Madonna" is any indication of what we have coming from the Beatles, I think now they know it too, and once again the Beatles are listening to the Beach Boys – as they always have.

I think the simpler you are the more you let people get into their own heads. I don't know if that's some kind of a rule that we've been taught, or just what it is, but I find that true with me. Like, I've always felt that real psychedelic music, for instance, could be found in the first Dylan albums – PAUL: The more you channel your actions in one direction, the more force there is behind what you're doing. DAVID: Right. PAUL: I just want to watch out for people drawing the conclusion that the new Dylan album means you shouldn't have been playing all those instruments after all, which is just nonsense. If they listen to the Byrds album then they'll understand that, but . . . and that's what a lot of people think "simplicity" means. It's like vindication for all the guys with their guitars.

DAVID: I still think simplicity is the highest form of art. Simplicity is unique for each person who's involved in it; I mean there's no hard line as to what is simple; and what is simple to Brian is not necessarily simple for Dylan, and what is simple for him is not necessarily simple for the Stones, or the Doors . . . very funny, the other day Morrison made a comment that really made me feel good: his favorite musician is Brian Wilson. PAUL: Jim? DAVID: Mm-hm. PAUL: That's amazing. DAVID: And one of his favorite albums is *Wild Honey*. I mean he really got into it . . . And what was even more mind-blowing about that particular situation was that Jim immediately hipped, or I guess had always been hip to the fact of Brian's involvement with humor. We happened to get into a conversation about humor, and the importance of humor, and immediately Jim mentioned Brian. And *Wild Honey*. And I think he, I believe if I remember correctly he was talking about *Wild Honey* and Brian in terms of direct, forceful statements.

PAUL: Well, the Doors have done essentially only one thing in their whole career; the Doors have done what other people are figuring out how to do, in other words make single statements, unify everything, and make it all come out of that one piece of art. And the Doors' problem therefore has been that people waited for something else to happen, and didn't get it, and weren't always satisfied with more of the same great stuff. So it's going to be very interesting that they're now thinking about other things.

DAVID: It's very strange; and it seems that only in music we find this, this need to keep changing. I directly relate it to painting – we're in a situation right now where everybody has to be a Picasso, everyone has to get into new things with every painting. And uh . . . Rembrandt certainly had his one style, Modigliani had his one style, most of the recognized great painters pretty much stuck within the one style that they found to be their own. PAUL: There's a perfectly good reason: it's the newspaper aspect of rock. It just comes out, you know; a new album comes out three months, five months, after the last one, and you're conscious of it as a part of right now. Maybe you won't be ten years from now, but right now you're conscious that this is The New Album, and you're thinking that way. DAVID: Yeah, that makes a lot of sense to me. If the recording artist were in the same position as the painter, let's say, and recorded continually as the painter paints continually, I think that he would very quickly come to his particular thing and stay with it, whereas, you're right, recording an album right now is really an event. It's an event for the record label, it's an event for the artist, it's an event for the people who are waiting for the album. PAUL: Everybody goes through their little birth sequence. DAVID: Everyone thinks that this next one has to be something more than the last one. And I think we've really gone through it. It's just ridiculous, this fantastic searching that everyone goes through trying to come up with something new, as if that were important. PAUL: People are just beginning to settle down now.

Like I know what's happened to me: I've finished this book, or I will have when we finish this conversation, and I no longer . . . somehow, although I was never conscious that I felt it before, I now know that I don't feel any more responsibility – which I did – in terms of writing about rock and roll. I don't know to whom . . . But from now on I can sit down and anything I write about rock and roll is just for fun, for me; 'cause I've got other things to do, I've proven myself in this area. Whereas before . . . an example of this is I'm only now getting to the point where I don't feel I have to listen to everything that comes out that's good. I never listened to everything that came out, I never got into that hang-up. But now I'll even know that a record is good, and I will get around to it; but if I feel like listening to nothing but old Who singles for the next two weeks, that's what I'll do. I don't worry about having people looking at me funny 'cause I don't know where it's at, or whatever.

Okay, so for a rock group, now, consider how difficult it has been to be in a field where you have to be a part of what's happening, and every month they change the rules. I think we might just now be getting to the point where a group can feel they don't have to do this or have to do that. Up to now, there were always responsibilities; and I think they were always vague and felt by the person rather than imposed from outside.

DAVID: And it's very strange, because Elvis has been there for eleven years, showing everyone that they didn't have to do anything that . . . he's been doing his one thing for eleven years! And they've been buying it. And every rock group has said, "Yeah. Elvis. Elvis." You can't talk to any person in the music scene who doesn't hold Elvis at a certain level. And he's never changed. He's always been Elvis. And uh . . . And I think Brian is always gonna be Brian! I think Brian is really on the road now; that's why I'm anxious for his next album, 'cause I think the next album is gonna be the solidification of what he's been doing. *Pet Sounds* was *Pet Sounds*; and I think *Smile*, looking back now that I've gotten into *Wild Honey*, I think *Smile* would've been an extension of *Pet Sounds*, that Brian probably figured was not necessary.

PAUL: Ahh. I don't think you can use the word "necessary" in relation – that's another thing I mean about responsibility, the point at which we really start breathing a little easier, is the point at which we don't – DAVID: We don't put all the people on our shoulders. PAUL: All of a sudden we don't have to think that anything's necessary in terms of the art. DAVID: That's easy to trace with Brian. Until *Pet Sounds*, and everyone started paying attention to Brian, he was making music. He was making music that he felt he had to make, and all of a sudden he was surrounded by all these people who kept saying, "You're a leader, you've really got the responsibility, look what you're doing," and I think he got into that for a while. PAUL: And he did it to himself, too; he started thinking of *Pet Sounds* as a breakthrough, the work of a new person . . . DAVID: Well, he allowed himself to fall prey to what was going on, it was Othello and Iago, in a sense, and then all of a sudden I think he realized that that's not where he's at. Where he's at is to make the music that he wants to make, whatever it may be, whether it's "Help Me, Rhonda" or "In My Room" or "God Only Knows" or whatever. "Darlin'." *Wild Honey*. When I listen to *Wild Honey* I really remember Brian sitting at that piano by himself just screaming his soul out. And he doesn't have to do any more than that. For anyone who likes Brian that's where it's at. *Wild Honey should* be celebrated. You were right.

PAUL: People have to relax. There are too many albums out right now to listen to, there's too much good music to appreciate, there are too many other things to do to be able to get your life in balance at all, in that way. I don't care if people read their issues of *Crawdaddy!* when they come out or six months later. I don't care how recently an album was released. This is not a letting go, it's a sitting back. DAVID: Sitting back and relaxing. PAUL: And as it starts influencing the business itself, it should really make a lot of musicians feel better.

DAVID: I think it's going to be very good for the business. Just in the few people that I associate with, they're more solid now into the area of recording albums that are musical, as opposed to the next major production album. There's a whole bunch of excitement going on, because everyone is really relaxing. I mean all the artists are now saying, "Thank God, we can get back to our music, we don't have to search and struggle and anticipate a $50,000, five-month-in-the-making record." And it's gonna be beautiful.

PAUL: What did you learn from Mike Love? DAVID: I didn't learn anything from Mike Love, I just learned something about Mike Love. I was at the last Love – this is a very funny thing, the way everything happened; we were cutting two more sides for what we thought at that time would be the next Love single. I was having my head blown sitting there, watching Love really getting it together, sounding better than they've ever sounded and being happier than I've ever seen them in a recording studio. And right in the middle of this, Mike Love and Al Jardine walked in, and I hadn't seen them in an awful long time.

I left the studio for a moment to talk to Mike and Al, and I noticed the fantastic physical difference in Mike, a real peace thing happening to him. He was very exuberant about his experiences with the Maharishi and transcendental meditation – which is something that I am not into nor do I really understand, except for the fact that I have talked to a lot of people lately who have been exposed to both the Maharishi and his philosophy and who have really changed, are really peaceful with themselves. And Mike was just bubbling over about the Beach Boys' involvement with the Maharishi and their plans to leave for India and also their plans for the tour that I believe they have now set up with the Maharishi.

But the incredible thing was the change in Mike. He was so calm, so quiet, so gentle and happy around the eyes and very genuine. The first thing that came to my mind while he was talking, as I was standing there listening to him, was the last time we were together doing the interview and I was talking about the negative things that used to go down between Brian and Mike. And I was wondering if that still existed or if they had found their niche together, 'cause Brian has been into the Maharishi for so long. I have no way at this point of knowing what that means . . . unless I can see them together. I'm waiting for Mike to come back 'cause he said we would get together when he came back and talk about some things. PAUL: It would seem that the Beach Boys are getting back together. DAVID: It sure seems that way, doesn't it? PAUL: Because I'm sure that the Beach Boys, the other Beach Boys are very happy with this album too. DAVID: I would think so. PAUL: It's the solution to a lot of problems.

I love the way we can see all sorts of answers now, and we couldn't see any, to the *Wild Honey* question, at the beginning, I mean when we were really looking. This has to do, I think, with what a breakthrough is. A breakthrough is really a move from two dimensions into three dimensions. DAVID: Well the last time we talked, when we heard *Wild Honey*, that was still very new to me . . . I guess I couldn't see the trees for the forest. I was expecting so much and it was all there but I didn't recognize it. And it took a couple of things to all of a sudden remember, and your phone conversation, and *John Wesley Harding* and watching this whole transitional thing happening and the going back and whatever it is that's going on. And all of a sudden realizing –

PAUL: This interview, to me – well, it's first of all of course a study of Brian Wilson, an attempt at evoking him for a lot of people, a look into who he is. And in the context of my book, the only deep look into who the artist is in relation to the music, an attempt to capture that. And it's full of dead ends; I mean I like it partly for that reason. DAVID: Yeah, there are a lot of dead ends. PAUL: Like we spent basically the first two installments as it appears in the magazine talking about how *Smile* got lost and what was gonna happen and in fact the end of the second installment is a cliff-hanger, you know about is Brian going to do it or not? Even though the answer was right in front of us. And what I would hope is that through this, that this interview would become for people like a story about not just who the artist is a little but who the listener is. DAVID: That would be beautiful, if the listener can be made aware of himself through anything that's happening here . . . it would be like the frosting on the cake. PAUL: We're all listeners, which we forget, just like our economic system falls apart because we forget that we're all consumers. Everybody. It was supposed to work on that principle.

The same thing here, the artist is himself a listener – oh, we talked about Brian not listening to other people's records much and that sort of thing, but – let's not just say listener but . . . we don't have a word for it, a listener and a watcher, person-who-experiences . . . there's an intake, for instance we talked about Brian's – DAVID: A massive intake, I hope in the interview that that comes across, because as incredibly strong as he is in terms of output, he's equally strong in input. Just massive consumption, of the world and everything. When I said that Brian doesn't listen much, that was really erroneous on my part. He listens, he listens with simplicity, I mean he gets it immediately and he gets the

81

whole thing right away, he gets it on mass consumption and just boom! he soaks it all in and it's digested and he listens the way I think we would like people to listen, everyone to listen. He doesn't listen with the critical thing up front, he just listens to whatever it is, just the way he sees things for whatever they are and then they form their, uh, whatever it is that forms is automatically formed.

PAUL: A number of years ago, at a time when I was still thinking of wanting to be a writer and all, I flashed on a concept of myself as wanting to do three things – experiencing, you know, taking in whatever was out there, understanding it, that's the second part, and then communicating it to people. And I recently came back to that, to that concept. You could talk about intake, digestion, and production.

DAVID: That really is so simple.

But how few people really get all those three things going equally. Most people try to concentrate on the middle thing, they try to understand everything without experiencing it, and then too few of them have the capacity or the knowledge of how to get it out, how to communicate it. PAUL: You know, I think the middle thing is the natural one, digestion is the natural one, so you can't figure out how to do it; that's why we're against interpretation or whatever. It's really simply because we know that if you've got things coming in the way you want them, good things are happening to you, you're getting involved in what you want to be involved in, and if you know what you want to produce, whether it's a kind of writing or music or whatever, then the link, digestion, you pretty much – it's what's called doing things by ear or sailing by the seat of your pants. You get very skilled at having things come in and then without really thinking about it moving them through your head, through your life, your artistic person towards the point where they come together and emerge as something whole. DAVID: A lot of people fake it. PAUL: Yeah, they take it in, and they let it sit there for a while, and then they toss it out. DAVID: Right, they don't try to understand it at all, and they don't even really take it all in, but they *try* to get it all out, they try to foist it upon everyone else.

PAUL: Well, you know what's a good essay on this subject? The liner notes of *John Wesley Harding*. DAVID: Oh, the liner notes of *John Wesley Harding*! I played the album so many times before I even got into the liner notes at all, I didn't even read them, and then one night I was walking into the kitchen and the album cover was sitting on the table and I grabbed it and just casually started reading it. And then I had to just sit down, and I got into that thing, and I was on the floor laughing. Such a beautiful thing to happen all of a sudden one dumb lonely night, to have that thing happen in my brain.

PAUL: Listening is another digestion operation, the concept of relaxing is a move towards understanding how to digest. Remember the Byrds' song "5D"? Where he talks about, "Just relax and feel it around you." DAVID: You can't really get it without relaxing. The work comes later; I think the work comes in between the knowledge and the output. You have to train yourself to observe, or train yourself to experience totally, to hear, it is definitely a training process. But after you as an individual get to that point, then you have to relax. Let it happen to you. PAUL: Let yourself function, because you've become some sort of a functioning thing, and you can just let it work.

Well, this is the – the relaxed part of the interview. DAVID: We've really digressed from Brian, haven't we? But he allows you to do that. (Laughter.) Brian allows you to go on your own trip. I would like to comment, though, before this is all over, about the picture you used in the first installment. I don't know how, who, what, or any of those situations on that picture [Linda Eastman took the photo], but that has to be the best picture I've ever seen of Brian. Ever. That's . . . so *perfect* for what was happening in that interview – that picture tied in with the very last thing we were talking about, which was, if you remember, the physical thing. Brian would always get that look on his face, or he'd always yawn – when it was time to stop

83

talking about something, and he would want you to know that, he would yawn. And you knew after a while that, okay, it's all over, now we go play or something – he may catch you right in the middle of a sentence too, he'll yawn, that's all. Maybe tomorrow we'll pick up, but for right now, no more talk, time to do something. And it just blew my mind to see that particular picture. 'Cause that's so perfect. PAUL: Well, the way things happen is always very complicated and strange, and not always relevant to the fact that they do happen . . . that was the only photo available . . .

See, given that we have a new attitude towards the records now, as a result of *Wild Honey* and *John Wesley Harding* and whatever, and that we've progressed or broken through to the artist appreciating what he's doing, and us appreciating what's he's doing, on a much less self-conscious, formal kind of basis, a much more immediate basis, ah, something that's going to happen, whether we try to do it or not, is that we're going to change around our idea of who the artist is. That's "us" as listeners. In other words, the way that Bob Dylan would have been written about and thought of as a superstar at one time has already changed a great deal. But I don't think it's gotten to the point yet where anybody really has an exact idea of who Bob Dylan is. Which they did when he was a superstar – I'm not saying they were right, they had an exact idea, that's all. And probably in a few more months we'll all be well set in our new fantasy of who Bob Dylan is. The fantasy is unavoidable – the point is, our concept of who the artist is is changing. And what I want to do is sort of round off our story of Brian by going right at it and saying, your saying who Brian Wilson now seems to be.

DAVID: Brian now seems to be the Brian Wilson that I first met in the early days of "Good Vibrations," before it was finished, and also the same Brian Wilson that I knew from two o'clock in the morning to seven o'clock in the morning when it was just Brian and I sitting in the living room talking. It was the Brian Wilson away from all the hoopla, before he started perhaps listening to what people were saying about him. A very simple person, um . . . again, "simple," we get to that word . . . a very direct person, a person who really knew who he was, both as a person and as an artist. A person who had the incredibly complex mechanisms pretty much under control. He would go into a studio without fear, because he had confidence, in himself and in his art. He had things pretty much – he had everything in perspective, he had eliminated everything that was unnecessary. Brian was really – people used to really think Brian was a simple person in the true sense of the word simple, because he just didn't need all of the fooforall that a lot of us get hung up in, that we don't get hung up in any more, some of us . . . He was the artist, Brian was an artist, he was an artist who knew his art, as he is right now. PAUL: And then he discovered the word "artist." DAVID: Right.

Whatever agony, and God knows there is a lot with him, whatever loneliness, whatever indecision that goes on, that is necessary in a person like Brian, all that was safely tucked away inside of him, that was his own world. He had learned somewhere along the line how to keep that inside of him, and how to eliminate all those things in his surroundings that would cause him to lose control. I think he's there right now. I think he went through a terrible period, for a while, and then into a period of isolation, and then the clear light came to him and I think he has now gone back to where he was just previous to *Pet Sounds*. PAUL: Gone ahead to where he was. DAVID: And he must be very happy right now. He must be as happy as Brian Wilson can be happy. He's probably exploring all the numerous realms of humor, which is again his big thing. I don't think he's hung up.

That's the whole thing. Brian, when I first met Brian he was the most un-hung-up person I'd ever met. And that's why people couldn't relate to him, because it was during the time when you really had to be hung up to get it on, and Brian just was not. I don't think he's hung up now. He must be in the studio exactly the way he was then: just get in there and get it

85

on, get it done, and get it out, and go on to the next thing. And that's what *Wild Honey* is to me, at this point. And "Darlin' " is just the essence of the Brian that I knew; it's doing the thing, it's doing his thing, it's doing Brian Wilson's thing. Come hell or high water, no concern really for what they out there think. It's what Brian Wilson thinks. He has to be grooving with the guys, and they have to be grooving with him again. It's gotta be a unified situation.

I don't know. You know, I try to relate Brian to other figures or other people, to try to get a comparison thing or some kind of a mirror thing happening . . . for some reason I keep coming up with images like Rembrandt. I don't know who the hell Rembrandt was, except for what we read and what we can get, or what I can personally get from looking at his works, collective works. An artist who is totally sure of what he is doing, who believes in what he is doing, who is conscious of what's going on around him, probably more conscious than the great mass of other people, but unconcerned while being concerned – not letting it get in his way. Being able to listen to someone else's music and say, "Yeah; all right." You know, "That's groovy. That's groovy for them. But I'm not in a competition scene with them, I'm doing my thing." And he is indeed doing his thing. And he's going to capture, or recapture, a lot of people. He's going to get a whole entire new audience, he's going to be able to get the new generation that's coming in now to the music thing, he's going to get back a lot of us old-timers . . .

And he's not concerned, he can't be concerned with his influence in the music business. Any guy who could dress the way Brian dressed, you *know* is not hung up with appearance, is not hung up with what others are doing. He's into his thing, whatever makes him comfortable he'll do. Whatever he wants to do at the moment. He doesn't have to sit and ponder and worry and get hung up and inactive because he's so strung out. He knows what's gonna happen and he's doing it. And in his doing it will be accomplished. It's an emancipation, an artistic

86

emancipation that not many people have. It comes from confidence and it also comes from a kind of naive thing that artists have, good artists have; they're really naive. "Hey, my stuff is good." Which is beautiful. Without that, forget it. It's egoless, in terms of being a nonconscious thing . . .

PAUL: Brian, I think, is out of time. DAVID: Brian has always been out of time. PAUL: And, uh, *Smile* took the shape of a concept which then had to be realized. And its failure to happen, well it was the slip, 'twixt the cup, you know, it was between the, what is it, the desire and the spasm falls the shadow or whatever Eliot goes on about . . . but it was because . . . at some later point in Brian's career, at some moment of even greater capability than he has now, *Smile* could have come to him and it would have gone right down. Well I guess "Surf's Up" came to him and it went right down, only then he didn't perceive it as being right down.

And delayed it, thought about it . . . DAVID: You just said something that really flashed me. It has to happen *immediately*, with Brian, the idea comes to the mind and he understands it instantly. Instinctively understands it. If Brian has to wait on something, pass. If he can't (snaps fingers) get it done like that, if he can't act upon it immediately and see it happening in front of his eyes, it's not gonna work. If he has to wait until morning, it's not gonna happen. That's what happened with *Smile*.

7

Friends

This particularly odd "review" was written for Crawdaddy! *after my conversation with David Anderle was published. It appeared in the September 1968 issue; very soon after that I left the magazine and did very little writing about music until 1974.*

Progress, claims GE, is their most important product. What do you suppose they mean by that? Forward movement of some kind, clearly; but forward movement in what context? Industrial progress? Then what would their reaction be if they started to realize that perhaps the next step in human progress is a step beyond the industrial, perhaps even a step incorporating but still *beyond* western science and its assumptions of causality? Would General Electric manufacture and sell divining rods if they turned out to be effective at locating underground sources of water in dry areas? Is General Electric committed to some old-fashioned (non-progressive) concept of technological progress, or are they really ready to spring for *human* progress? I mean, will they move forward even if it means moving out of their starting context?

The Beach Boys, of course, are moving forward all the time.

Each Beach Boys album since *Pet Sounds* has been (or seemed) a little less sophisticated. Retrogression? Not at all, but to prove that, we'd better decide what "forward" is.

Forward is the direction in which time moves. It's kind of like "out," which is the direction in which cosmic matter moves. There is no possibility of reversal inherent in this movement, nor even of angular shift. Those concepts have no meaning. Can a line stretching from zero towards infinity turn around? At best, it would no longer be a straight line. So "forward" is a description of how time moves, just as outward might describe how space moves, if we think of "space" the concept rather than the objects that move about *within* space.

Now, "forward" as applied to the Beach Boys must have to do with their relationship to time. Do they move forward in time (or rather, with it)? Yes, of course, everybody does. Do they make progress? To answer that, we must consider their work as existing in time, and ask: is there a real movement (if there is, it couldn't be anything but forward) from the Beach Boys' earlier creations to their more recent ones? Not, do they get better? (That would require a highly subjective judgment. I, personally, do not think they get better; I feel they are as great now, or conversely, were as great then. I don't favor any particular period.) Rather, do they incorporate the past in the present? Do they seem to learn? Do they operate out of some kind of awareness of past accomplishment and failure, or are they striking out anew from the beginning, the origin, every time? The question is, is there some kind of real expansion evident in the achievements of the Beach Boys as time goes on, something that would justify our considering one album as a step forward from a previous one?

This is very difficult to answer; it breaks down into a matter of subjective judgment no matter how we try to avoid that. I would say that, taking the various albums the Beach Boys have done and shuffling them, it is not necessarily evident that there are "more advanced" and "less advanced" albums. They have reached different audiences at various times. And these audiences, therefore, like to say they were only good up to this point, or since that point ("Good Vibrations" is one popular dividing line). However, I would argue that, from the point of view of the longtime listener who has taken them pretty much for what they are, the Beach Boys have covered more distance than almost any other group in rock.

Can I explain that statement? I hope so. It must be remembered that the consistent listener himself moves forward with time; he or she heard *Pet Sounds* in 1966 and *Smiley Smile* in 1967 and *Friends* in 1968. So each new record the group releases may well seem to her or him not merely another piece of plastic to be measured against past pieces, but rather the most recent advance of a continually expanding body of work (a glacier, or a tree, is a good analogous example of an object in movement that moves only in a forward direction and without leaving its point of origin).

In terms of the listener, he feels himself moved *further* (at least I do) by each new album the Beach Boys produce. This is not true with most groups, even very good ones: generally speaking, they get into something good and then turn out great quantities of the same good stuff, variations on the original theme, until at last they get bored and move onto something new (after maybe three perhaps great but basically stagnant albums). The Beach Boys, in their work since *Pet Sounds* and I believe throughout their careers, have been pressing constantly on, relentless in dissatisfaction, in the need to express more and more of themselves (as opposed to the need for expressing the same thing more and more effectively).

So what happens to the listener is this: he is familiar with the Beach Boys, he likes them, meaning he enjoys most of what they've put out and rather expects that they will continue to create worthwhile (to him) music. He sees a new Beach Boys album in the shop window, purchases it, takes it home and plays it and lo and behold, *he cannot relate!* Is this the same Beach Boys I know and love? he wonders, knowing full well it is, the voices certainly sound familiar, but somehow this is not what he expected. It is not more of the same. It is something entirely new, as though the group had just appeared on the scene and expected to be listened to with no preconceptions whatsoever.

Not more of the same. And as a result, it is extremely difficult for the listener to say whether or not he likes the record. On first listening, it appears to have no relevance, either to him or to his idea of who the Beach Boys are.

But (I hope) he continues to play the record. And slowly but surely he finds one song and then another quite stuck inside his mind; he hears the music in his head as though his mind were a portable radio and the song were being picked up by him directly as waves in the air. He finds himself more and more deeply involved in the album, until he hears each separate song with great pleasure and feels an affection for the album itself. Quite unconsciously, he has come to like the record, and now he may say, after the fact, that it's good, he likes it, the Beach Boys have done it again.

Do you know what has happened? His head has been opened. A whole new thing, which he responded to not at all at first, has been added to his consciousness, he now responds to this strange music warmly and with sensitivity, and he is not at all the same listener he was before he bought the album. He has, *bien sur*, made progress. Progress not just within a context but beyond the contexts he as a listener was familiar with.

I have seen this happen, with *Pet Sounds, Wild Honey, Friends*. I've had it happen to me and I've spoken to many people who seem to have had the same experience. And I know very many people who've been turned off to the Beach Boys because they never got beyond that first baffling exposure to the album. It seems to me essential, if we are to stay as children, if we are to remain open to the world and what's in it, that we not take defensive postures, that we not hold on tighter to what we have whenever faced with something strange and new. Our only chance at escaping stagnation is to continue to grow almost in spite of every urge towards security and safety that we feel. True security can only be found in the ability to respond fully to any situation.

So let us praise the Beach Boys for their progress. *Friends* is not the least bit like *Wild Honey*, though it retains *Wild*

Honey's achievement of the casual and the everyday and the immediate (and explores these things somewhat further). It is not at all *Smiley Smile*, although its explorations of organ sound as it relates to melody and to the human voice continue. *Friends* is, furthermore, no return to *Pet Sounds*, though it might please those who have been seeking in the Beach Boys the calm, the softness of *Pet Sounds* (*Friends* lacks *Pet Sounds*' passion – which you can find even more in *Wild Honey* – but it is in many ways both more comforting and more adventurous). *Friends* is merely a new Beach Boys album, and as such both the successful expression of their current interests and feelings and a real step forward on the part of the Beach Boys' music in general. Not because this is a better album than any before, but because Beach Boys music and Beach Boys listeners' perceptions of music are now that much further developed – more sophisticated, through being deeply sensitive to apparently simpler stuff – than they ever were before. An important product indeed.

8

New Packages
(*Endless Summer, Wild Honey & 20/20*)

From Crawdaddy! *(I hadn't been the editor since '68, but they still let me write record reviews), November 1974.*

Ah, seventh heaven. Capitol has been repackaging the Beach Boys for a long time, but they haven't done a good job of it since *Best Of* Volumes I, II and III, all long gone now. This time they hit pay dirt: *Endless Summer* is the best single early Beach Boys package ever, well-programmed and including almost every track that one could wish for (if one could choose only twenty from the pre-*Pet Sounds* era).

Plus, simultaneously, a Reprise re-release of two glorious albums from the '67-'69 period, which, I discovered when I went out to rebuild my collection (too much travelling leaves you bereft – where is my copy of the Shades of Blue singing "Oh How Happy," now that I need it?), have been selling in record shops for fifteen to twenty dollars each!

Both double albums are required listening for anyone who hopes to grok American rock 'n' roll – or, for that matter, America – and they're also guaranteed to let a lot of pleasure into even the darkest life. (You probably knew that already.) I was delighted to see *Endless Summer* rocket into the Top 20 albums, and even *Wild Honey & 20/20,* which contains four or five "hits" but none that were really big, is solidly in the Top 100. How reassuring to think that after all these years

95

(twelve or thirteen) the world is still full of Beach Boys lovers.

Wild Honey and *20/20* are just the same great records they always were, and it's nice to have them back again. Surprisingly nice. A lot of old favorites lose their edge when you listen to them again, except for special moments once in a while. But these old Beach Boys albums (I don't think of them as old, but my God! It's been seven years since I first puzzled over the lack of sophistication of *Wild Honey*) are as pleasant and rewarding as the first time around. Better, maybe, because we are set free of the strange anxieties of those days: "It's good, but it's not *Smile...*" or "Does this mean that the new direction is simplicity?" Now it's just music: lovable, recognizably better than most of what is being released now (any now), clearly destined to live forever.

Like all Beach Boys albums, repeated listenings turn these two into little symphonies. (*Pet Sounds* was famous for that, but the effect was equally striking on *The Beach Boys Today* and *Shut Down Volume II.*) *Wild Honey* is a remarkable tribute to the *feeling* of r&b music, the exuberant vocals (the first BBs album dominated by solo vocal performances) pushing against those astonishing tracks (listen to the bass!), filled with enough musical ideas for a half-century of pop recording. It's a Brian Wilson composition straight through, with Mike Love's silly, grin-provoking lyrics offering Brian support and direction. A home studio job, and if you can get those ecstatic "Country Air" echoes in your own mansion, why go down to Sunset Strip ever again?

20/20 is every brother getting into the act, a trend begun on *Friends.* Al Jardine and Bruce Johnston get their own songs, too. Talent busting out all over the place, and somehow it all holds together. One of the mellowest BBs albums, delightful listening.

Endless Summer takes us back to the days when each two-minute song was a conscious masterpiece of mass-communication and the Beach Boys' identity derived from individual songs rather than albums. (In the middle period it definitely derived from albums, climaxed by the curious success of *Surf's Up* – a success seemingly derived from the delayed media impact of the awe people like me had felt five years earlier when we listened to the unfinished tracks from *Smile*. The song "Surf's Up" had actually been heard by a great many people, on a Leonard Bernstein TV special, and somehow it all added up to five years of expectation that was not really satisfied, but anyway released (free at last!), when *Surf's Up* became an album – the only pretentious album the Beach Boys ever made.) Now the Beach Boys' identity derives from their concert tours and long-time track record. People respect them and love them and don't care if there's a hit single again or how good the latest album is.

Oh, the early days. "Wendy." "Don't Worry Baby." "The Warmth of the Sun." "Be True to Your School." The names themselves have magic, and it's not nostalgia for that time in our lives, but rather remembrance of individual ecstatic musical experiences. Those melodies, those voices – something like "The Warmth of the Sun" is as close as I can imagine to contemporary holy music. Listen to it. We mortals weren't meant to experience such perfect art. It'll drive you out of your mind.

The first 25 seconds of "California Girls" are rivalled only by the intro to "Gimme Shelter." The Beatles at their best can barely compete with the structuring of "Fun, Fun, Fun" or "I Get Around"; and no one has ever approached the economy of "Shut Down" (the musical, cultural, and philosophical history of western civilization in one minute and fifty seconds). The Beach Boys are masters; if anyone has heard music this consistently brilliant anywhere else in modern times, let me know about it special delivery.

Incidentally, I can't say how pleased I am that for seemingly the first time ever, Capitol managed to put out a repackage that didn't include "409." I trust the success of these two sets means we can count on *Friends & Smiley Smile* from Reprise within the next ten months or so . . . God knows we need it. If I could make a request, do you think you could fit "Break Away" and "Celebrate the News" on there somewhere? *Pet Sounds* is also available from Reprise, dear reader, FYI, and yes it's as good as they say. I wish I (once again) had a copy of every BBs album, including *Christmas* and *Stack-o-Tracks*, but all in good time . . . Meanwhile I'm very happy with what we do have, and as soon as I stop typing I'm going to start listening again.

9

Live in New York,
September and November 1974

Here are two fragments recording my impressions at the time of a couple of Beach Boys concert appearances. The first, just a paragraph, is from a review I wrote for the Soho Weekly News of a massive outdoor concert Sept 8, 1974 at Roosevelt Raceway on Long Island, featuring Jesse Colin Young, Joni Mitchell, Crosby, Stills, Nash & Young, and the Beach Boys. The second, about a mid-November show at Madison Square Garden in New York City, is a page I found in my files. I imagine it was a first stab at an article for The Soho News that turned into just a record review (see chapter 10).

The Beach Boys are exuberant performers who happen to have some of the best material ever written by anyone. Their set (which I squeezed up close to the stage for part of; it's a tossup – fun to be up front watching, but the sound is better further back) went from one peak to another: "I Can Hear Music," "Sunny California," "Long Promised Road" (Carl just incredible on keyboards), "Don't Worry Baby," "Sail on Sailor" . . . It was religious, ecstatic; the whole crowd seemed in love with the Beach Boys, singing along, dancing, not letting them off the stage. James Guercio (producer of Chicago) played bass, and Mike Love wore a green Caribou Ranch shirt, white pants, a silver belt, Panama hat with multicolor brim, and a double string of puka.

The Beach Boys are the oldest established permanent floating rock act in America, (they haven't missed a year since

1962). They also make the best music America has to offer. This has long been true on record, but I'm beginning to think it may be true on stage, too. At Madison Square Garden last week, the Beach Boys were magnificent. By the time they did their final numbers, the whole building was shaking.

They played for an hour and three quarters, and it was straight-out ecstacy for almost everyone in that audience (the place was packed; 99% of capacity). All that beauty in all those BBs songs is not only captured live but is improved on – the sound is bigger, fuller. Imagine "The Warmth of the Sun" fully realized and ten times larger than on the record. (Mike explained that he and Brian wrote the song early in the morning after JFK was shot.) Imagine 10,000 people singing "Surfer Girl."

The audience roared for the big hits, but they also jumped to their feet shouting for songs that were never even singles: "Catch a Wave," "Feel Flows." It was not a '60s nostalgia night. It was we-love-the-Beach-Boys'-music night, and the group was clearly basking in the glow. Carl was great. The audience were the real stars of the show (who'da thunk it, in Madison Square Garden?) – altogether one of the most positive and pleasurable big concert experiences I've ever had.

If you're not exactly clear what it is that makes so many people slightly fanatical about the Beach Boys, *Friends & Smiley Smile*, a new BBs reissue on Warner Brothers, may be just the record to convert you. These two albums were originally released in 1967 and 1968. Together they make it very clear that music's potential to make people feel good has been explored only superficially so far in rock music – these two albums suggest so many new ideas for what rock could be.

10

Friends & Smiley Smile
(the reissue)

This one appeared in The Soho Weekly News *(New York City), November 28, 1974.*

This is the third double-album of reissued Beach Boys recordings released so far this year. *Endless Summer*, on Capitol, was a magnificent collection of early hit singles and surf/sun/car-oriented album tracks, the definitive First Era Beach Boys package and a $2 million seller thanks to heavy TV advertising. *Wild Honey & 20/20* was another summer package, offering two excellent and long-unavailable albums from the Second Era of the Beach Boys (1966–1969). *Friends & Smiley Smile* is more of the same (two Second Era LPs packaged together), and you may well wonder, isn't this getting to be too much of a good thing?

No. The Beach Boys are the only major rock group (exception: the Kinks) whose best work has been long unavailable; they are also probably the only '60s rock group whose popularity has been steadily growing throughout the '70s (possible exception: The Who) as a result of their constant touring and thanks to a real word-of-mouth spreading awareness of Beach Boys music among people who were too young or too old to notice when the group first captured public attention.

This new Beach Boys audience was very much in presence at

the group's Madison Square Garden concert last week. The crowd that virtually filled the Garden (99% of capacity despite very little publicity) was not a "Solid Gold" crowd trying to recapture their adolescence, nor was it a crowd turning out for a pop Event a la Elton John. Rather it was a sea of enthusiastic young people come to hear joyous, spirited music, and music is what they got – between the superb performances and surprisingly full sound of the group and the wondrous mood of the audience (jumping to their feet and shouting when the group began to sing "The Warmth of the Sun," a classic but never a hit single), it was one of the finest concerts I ever attended. During the endless encores it was possible to stand still and feel the whole building shaking. Some 80 kids joined hands and danced in a half-circle around the huge outer circumference of the audience area. "And she'll have fun, fun, fun now that Daddy took the T-bird away-y-y . . ."

Friends and *Smiley Smile* (this new package is simply the original LPs, from '68 and '67 respectively, without their original covers, in a gatefold jacket with dull art and intelligent liner notes) are two of the most intimate albums ever recorded by pop musicians. They are both home studio jobs (a throwback to the Beach Boys' first recordings, which according to legend were done in the Wilsons' garage), and the simplicity of style and performance on the two albums is in astonishing contrast to the wealth of musical innovation herein. Brian Wilson reminds one of J.S. Bach in the awesome purity and directness of his music, the seeming effortlessness and corniness with which he breaks every musical rule and throws open the doors of heaven.

Do I exaggerate? Judge for yourself. The humor and asonance of *Smiley Smile* may make it hard to get into at first, but *Friends* is totally accessible (providing you can suppress the initial feeling that it's far too simple-minded to be taken seriously). Play side one of *Friends* eight or ten times (it's short), and then take any one song ("Wake the World," perhaps) and listen to it alone several times. Then just let the song play in your mind, feel the pleasure of it, and gradually let yourself notice all the little things that are happening, musically, audibly, in that one minute and twenty-nine seconds. The changes, the progressions...! The perfect relationship between music and words (don't judge the words on their own, just let them hit you as part of the song, somehow the corniness transcends itself and becomes almost supernaturally comforting, amusing, satisfying).

Beach Boys mania is just a natural extension of love for music. It takes a while to break down our instinctive resistance to simplicity and genius (I resisted fiercely until the summer of 1966, when *Pet Sounds* got me), but eventually we give in, and that's why there is a growing market for Beach Boys albums, Beach Boys reissues, Beach Boys concerts, six years after their last AM radio hit.

Friends & Smiley Smile includes "Heroes and Villains," *the* favorite BBs song for many of us fanatics, and 22 other short and wondrous recordings. No other 1974 record (except the other BBs reissues) comes close to it in richness of musical ideas, modest intimacy, or musical beauty. Pass it by if you like; but you'll only be delaying your own rediscovery of the joy of listening.

11

Brian Wilson

In 1988, Sire Records released the first Brian Wilson solo album, called Brian Wilson, *and tainted by the presence of the svengali doctor holding Brian prisoner and pulling his strings. Domenic Priore asked me in '88 to review the album for his book/magazine of Brian Wilson press clippings and related materials,* The Dumb Angel Gazette. *So this is what I wrote and Domenic published.*

I think I know what I want to say. It's about time. That is, time is what I want to say something about. "Brian's Back!" This seems like a simple statement, and it would be, except for the assumptions about time that are implicit within it. Everybody's asking, "Is he really back?", and for the most part their answer seems to be Yes. But the question I find myself wanting to ask is, "Was he ever gone?" And if so, was it him that went away . . . or was it me?

Time. Time has all these assumptions built into it. One is the illusion of progress. *Pet Sounds* is perceived as a maturing of Brian's art, and "Good Vibrations," which followed, is the extraordinary next step, and so the third point in the progression should be great beyond the powers of imagination. Some Beach Boys/Brian Wilson fans have been waiting ever since for this "progress," which got derailed one way or another, to resume.

Another time illusion is that the passage of time is important in itself. We keep reminding ourselves that this is Brian's first album in eleven years, or whatever, and the more we think about that gap, the more significant it seems. And indeed, speaking for myself, faithful and passionate Beach Boys fan though I was, I gave up somewhere along the way. *L.A.(Light Album)* did nothing for me, and the *Beach Boys* album of '85 or so was worse. So I decided the chances were small of ever hearing great music from Brian and/or the Boys again. And since I'd given up hope, Brian's 1988 solo album comes as a tremendous and wonderful shock. First, that it exists. And second, that this isn't a case of Brian straining awkwardly to sound like himself. In spite of all the effort, all the producers, Dr. L., a million dollars in expenses and so forth, somehow the album ended up an unpretentious, straightforward heaping plateful of true Brian music, different from but unmistakably cut from the same cloth as *Love You, Spring, Wild Honey, Sunflower, Shut Down Volume Two, Beach Boys Christmas Album,* and all those other wonders so easily overlooked by those (including me at times) who have chosen to portray Brian as a great constipated genius, sitting on the pot for twenty-two years trying to force out his masterwork.

There is no masterwork. There's just music. It flows naturally from the guy, despite all the obstacles that he (with help from the rest of us) puts in his own way. Flows like water. Once it flowed out like hit singles, a great succession of compact wonders full of delight, imagination, inspired musical invention. That material alone, incompletely summarized on *Endless Summer*, assures Brian's immortality as a musical presence and influence. Another time it flowed like naked, profound art, in the form of *Pet Sounds*. And at moments – notably "Good Vibrations," arguably "Surf's Up" and "Heroes and Villains" – it has flowed like tour-de-force aesthetic trailblazing, incandescence worthy of Van Gogh or a John Coltrane. But put aside all these major achievements, and sweep together what remains, and Brian Wilson is no less a genius or great composer or delightful musical friend; albums like *Spring* and *Wild Honey* may not be the sort of thing to make one rich or famous or even

106

fashionable, but the music in them, and in so many other Brian Wilson/Beach Boys creations, *is* enough to guarantee an artist's highest reward: eternal life. Hundreds of years from now, I guarantee it, people will be listening to *Beach Boys Love You* and "Breakaway" and "Marcella," or if they're not, will be absolutely flabbergasted and ecstatic to discover them.

What I like best about Brian's 1988 album is it has brought me back to a rich part of my life I'd forgotten about or written off as over and gone. I'm not talking about the past. I'm talking about something that's always present if I allow it to be: "Aren't You Glad" from *Wild Honey*, "In The Back of My Mind" from *Beach Boys Today*. Right now it's too soon to say for sure, but I don't doubt I'll be just as thrilled in years to come to rediscover "There's So Many' and "Melt Away." These are timeless treasures. And I'm the one who's come back to them. Brian never left.

12

"Fun, Fun, Fun"

This chapter and the next three are selections from a book I wrote in 1990 and 1991 called Rock and Roll: The 100 Best Singles. *The list was based on personal preference (What else is there?). And entries were arranged chronologically, not ranked from 1 to 100. As it worked out, the artists who had the most entries were The Beach Boys, The Beatles, Bob Dylan and the Rolling Stones, all tied for four singles each. The concept of the book was to write a hundred essays, each a cry of love, on the recurrent topic "What's so great about this one?"*

Always another wave coming along. Innocent and arrogant, the Beach Boys and the Beatles reinvented rock and roll (it had lost its identity between 1959 and 1962, a long, potentially deadly hiatus for a musical form that only became self-aware in 1955).

"Fun, Fun, Fun" starts by borrowing outright Chuck Berry's guitar intro from "Johnny B. Goode," a tribute as much as a rip-off. "Let your colors fly," the Beach Boys sang in their previous hit "Be True to Your School," and this purloined intro is just that, their pledge of allegiance to rock and roll and to the teenage nation for which it stands, with liberty (in the sense of un-self-conscious freedom) and good times for all.

If Elvis hadn't been drafted, if Buddy Holly hadn't died, if the payola scandal hadn't weakened the independent labels and stations and strengthened the corporate, conservative side of the music biz, maybe "rock and roll" would have grown up (and vanished) with the generation that discovered it. Instead, the subteens who grew up listening to the stuff got to reenact the rock revolution and make it their own. Second generation. A new teen nation replaces the old one. Play a few notes of the old guitar anthem to establish our legitimacy (and celebrate our roots), and let's get on with the party.

By defining rock and roll as a wide-open playground to be reinvaded by each new generation of teenagers, the Beach Boys and the Beatles (paradoxically) consolidated the gains of the previous rock era, establishing rock as a renewable resource, an ongoing, vital, enduring creative form. This is the permanent revolution that Jefferson and Marx could only dream of; and apparently it will last as long as successive "generations" of Western teenagers have lots of money to spend on music and few responsibilities to distract them.

"Fun, Fun, Fun" is a teen vignette in the Chuck Berry tradition, and stands as one of the all-time classics of the genre. Mike Love is underrated as a lyricist – "Well she got her daddy's car and she cruised through the hamburger stand now/Seems she forgot all about the library like she told her old man now" – now admit it, that's inspired. Brian Wilson's legendary inventiveness comes into play in the second and third verses, with the Greek chorus echoing each line ("you shouldn'ta lied now, you shouldn'ta lied"). Notice that the rebellious, fun-loving, fast-driving hero of the song is female. Notice that in every verse, every line except the last ends in "now," and it works! (One of the jobs of poetry is to capture not the actual words but the subjective impact of everyday speech.) Notice the understated, very specific, rhythmic sound of the words "fun, fun, fun" in the chorus, and the contrasting open-endedness of "away." Notice the easy, natural, wildly complex interplay between the voices and combinations of voices. Notice the neat double meaning in the second verse, "A lot of guys try to catch her," referring both to her elusive sexuality ("you look like an ace now") and her automotive ability ("you drive like an ace now"). Notice how Dad's futile attempt at discipline only serves to throw her (potentially) into "my" realm and bigger and better trouble. And I know you can't fail to notice one of the sweetest fade-outs ever, the brilliant ordinariness of the song totally transcended in two brief moments of soaring falsetto. Fun, indeed.

Innocence and arrogance. It's a delicate combination, and you can't fake any part of it. Get it just right, and the world will retaliate by throwing money and love and praise at you till they finally knock you off balance. But they can't take away the warmth of the sun and the spirit of independence that radiate from the grooves of this permanently revolving recording.

First release: Capitol 5118, January 1964

13

"I Get Around"/"Don't Worry Baby"

Another entry from Rock and Roll: The 100 Best Singles. *My rule was not to include both sides of a single unless I would include either side by itself. This 45 passed that criterion easily.*

At a certain level of intensity there is a complete lack of artifice. "Don't Worry Baby" is one of the pinnacles of rock and roll artistry because of its utter un-self-consciousness, its innocent, unmatchable power and sincerity. "Well, it's been building up inside of me for oh I don't know how long ..." This first line is self-referential; it describes the music we're hearing, the feelings that are being shared. What's been building up is the speaker's need to confess his anxiety to the listener. Intuitively, the listener knows that the singer/writer/producer (Brian Wilson) is speaking directly to him, to the person on the other end of the recording process. Brian's courage in sharing his "irrational" fears so honestly, so directly, is extremely affecting. "I don't know why but I keep thinking something's bound to go wrong." It is the power of his relationship with us that frightens him; yet he holds back none of that power here. The singer is totally present with his fears, naked before us, and his honesty is liberating; it gives the listener permission to be in touch with his (her) own anxieties, if my hero has them it's okay that I have them too. Having set this up, the song can go about its business, which is a) direct reassurance, and b) celebration of the female, the lover/mother, as the sole power that can (for the male) disperse the anxiety, make it bearable, allow me to face the world, keep breathing, go on with my work.

The rest of the lyrics, placing these feelings in the context of an impending car race, are awkward; their purpose is to put a fig leaf over the song's unprecedented intimacy, thus allowing it to be performed, released, listened to. And the awkwardness doesn't matter, because all we need to hear are those opening lines and the three words of the title; everything else is layers of sound – primarily vocal (lead and harmonies) but there are extraordinary instrumental (percussive) inventions here, too – so human and real and unspeakably beautiful that one sinks into them as into a cloudbank of heavenly reassurance, safety, harmony, love, surrendering all care, transported by the fullness and grace of these incomparable melodic and sonic textures.

These voices. Our awe at Brian's courage, musical imagination, and creative power should not cause us to overlook the importance of his constant inspiration and primary tool: the sound of these harmonizing voices, never more exquisite or personal than in the first few seconds of "Don't Worry Baby," like the comfort found walking by the edge of the ocean, waves breaking on our shore, invaluable natural resource.

"I Get Around," other side of the record and the Beach Boys' first #1 hit, is also a masterpiece. Two for the price of one. And the closer one listens, the more awe-inspiring it is. It's like the forerunner of some major new musical form that's still unexplored, even now, twenty-five years since this single was released. I'd go so far as to say that there's no way to represent on paper, with current notation, the lyrics, melody, rhythm, or arrangement of this song and come remotely close to what the listener actually hears and experiences. And of course it also flies in the face of conventional wisdom that anything so wildly experimental and avant-garde could be so popular, so dumb and friendly and instantly accessible. Un-self-consciousness is the key. Brian is so keen to please us, and to get into music certain feelings that he knows we feel, too, that he invents a whole new musical language without necess- arily realizing it, innocently finding the shortest distance from here to there, it's simple, bass guitar sounds like this, hand- claps here, sing this in this pitch, this in this other pitch and right here, lyrics vanish into falsetto here, chorus comes out of the clear blue sky with an attack like *this*, I'll keep the tempo, ready now? Let's go – And you look back and you've just crossed hyperspace. Hey that's cool. Listen, bring this master tape to Capitol and tell 'em it's the next single. And could you get us some milkshakes?

First release: Capitol 5174, May 1964

14

"Good Vibrations"

There has never been anything quite like this. It is a triumph of musical innovation in four or five different areas – song structure, instrumentation, techniques for recording the human voice, techniques for blending and separating (and creating musical transitions between) voices and groups of voices, and most of all new sounds plain and simple, amazing, beautiful, shocking, consciousness-expanding new sounds, like a painter creating new colors, incredible. And at the same time that it burst open vast realms of creative territory, uncompromisingly experimental, "Good Vibrations" was also an instant popular success, the best selling of all the Beach Boys' hit records. It was also the dominant inspiration and goad that drove the Beatles to create some of their most ambitious works. This single, following as it did the Beach Boys' triumphant *Pet Sounds* album, Bob Dylan's *Blonde on Blonde*, and the Beatles' *Revolver*, announced to whomever was interested that contemporary music had moved into a time of competitive creativity comparable to the rush of discovery and invention that marked the first flowerings of Impressionism and Cubism.

Brian Wilson is rock and roll's finest composer ever, and "Good Vibrations" is the most extraordinary of his compositions. (Not my favorite, however; perhaps it's a little *too* perfect.) Basically it expands on a single concept: the line "I'm picking up good vibrations," and the melodic and rhythmic phrase (nine beats) that goes with it. An echoing line is added, same music, different words – "She's giving me excitations."

This doubled phrase is then multiplied by four, a repeating chorus. The chorus becomes an implied round as a second set of voices comes in on the second line, laid over the first, singing a harmonic part that takes off from the original phrase – "good, good, good, good vibrations," barbershop quartet stuff, exquisite. The original line is only faintly audible when sung a third time, and the fourth time "good, good, good, good vibrations" takes over completely. A rhythmic shift, specifically a shift of momentum, has also taken place.

This is enclosed within a verse/chorus structure, with a bridging section and then an ending, like "River Deep, Mountain High," the primary outside influence on Brian in the writing of this song (his greatest influence, though, was the progressive development of his own music, as he continued to explore sound and composition by making one record after another – "Good Vibrations" is "Here Today" and "God Only Knows" from *Pet Sounds* multiplied times each other and shuffled together brilliantly, with a triple handful of new ideas thrown in).

So there are four parts: the first begins abruptly with the entry of Carl Wilson's great, soulful, vulnerable lead vocal, "I . . . I love the colorful clothes she wears." The musical track behind him is astonishingly beautiful, haunting, tactile, very simple at first but steadily and subtly building on itself, exploding after the musical transition that leads from the verse to that fabulous, ever-expanding chorus.

First part smacks right into second as the second verse starts – "Close my eyes" – before the last word of the chorus is quite finished. Verse; chorus; and then a sublime musical transition in the middle of the word "excitations" opens us out into part three, a remarkable musical and vocal bridge ("I don't know where but – "), heaven rock at its most transcendent ("ooh my my what a sensation"). Organ and tambourine take us out of the bridge and into the fourth and concluding segment, which begins with the repeated phrase "Gotta keep those lovin' good vibrations happenin' with her" and climaxes in an amazing "aaaahhh!", the official end of the song, after which everything is recessional, the explosive return of the "good good good good vibrations" part of the chorus, then the song's distinctive rhythm figure by itself, then a last burst of heaven rock (four lines of glorious rising harmony – "na na na na na, na-na-na"), with a bit of musical humor as final release and fade-out exit line.

Three minutes and thirty five seconds of genius. And it all reaches our ears as light and breezy and friendly as a warm spring afternoon.

First release: Capitol 5676, October 1966

15

"Heroes and Villains"

Another one of the 100 best singles. The "Mona" referred to is a (magnificent) 1957 single by Bo Diddley.

This is it. This is the record I love better than and indeed am more awestruck at than "Good Vibrations" (less perfect, but it goes so much further). In fact, if I had arranged this book in the foolish (but popular) hierarchical format, this record is one of the few that could have been a legitimate contender for first position. Right up there with "Mona." That tells you something, but damn if I know what.

Oh, actually, I suppose I do know what. Both are totally individualistic and at the same time alarmingly close to some kind of truly universal, pure human essence. In "Mona" it's the rhythms, and the singer's voice. In "Heroes and Villains" it's the rhythms of the voices, and of all the other sounds (voices of another sort). "Mona" is a single voice, speaking from deep in the under-conscious; "H & V" is a collective vocalization, speaking from the same deep place. Both have for me the unmistakable sizzle of a direct hook-up with higher awareness. Here is a taste of what reality really sounds like. Pipes of Pan. The voice of the avatar.

But don't let me spook you. It's a real pretty record, that's all. Astonishingly pretty. The words were written by a fellow named Van Dyke Parks, chosen by him for their sounds the way a mosaicist chooses stones for color and shape and relation to each other and magical resonance and then puts them together and they make a story, a picture. "I've been in this town so long that back in the city I've been taken for lost and gone and unknown for a long long time . . ." This is not mediocre poetry. Even if it weren't surrounded by such wonderful music, it'd be exquisite.

"Heroes and Villains" sounds, among other things, like a running brook. It sounds like nature looks and sounds and smells when we are in it and are truly in touch with the wonder of the natural world. It flows and dances. And, as that last word suggests, there is also a strong element of fantasy here. I am talking now not of the story but of the images conjured up by the music and by the sounds of the performance. As in "A Midsummer Night's Dream" we are caught up in the easy shift from the rapturously natural to the supernatural – "heroes and villains" because this is storybook stuff, a dance to the feelings evoked in a child's heart by the world of make-believe.

This record is a famous failure, in terms of its creators' impossible ambitions: it was to be the cornerstone of an evocative masterpiece that would have taken the sounds and feelings and wordplay explored herein, and extended them across a coherent album-length work, as complex and rich and perfect as anything ever attempted in composed or recorded music. Many additional fragments of "Heroes and Villains" exist on tape that may someday be released in their unfinished form. I'd love to hear them, and I love this legend of the album (called *Smile*) that flew too close to the sun. But the brightness of the myth can obscure what was in fact accomplished. All great works of art are failures in the sense that they reach for something that is ultimately beyond expression. It is not enough simply to reflect back the world that's known. What we love in art is the way it articulates and glorifies our own secret struggles to know and possess the unknowable.

We are most human, most mortal, when we are reaching for

something. And though we will never obtain what we reach for, our vulnerability at these moments of hyperextension is a gateway through which the most wondrous possessions can and do arrive. In "Heroes and Villains," the single Brian Wilson did have the courage and humility to complete and release in the form in which we know it, the one now playing on my phonograph, something comes to life that I have never heard on any other recording. Its presence is most obvious in the chorus ("Heroes and villains, just see what you've done done") as it moves from vocalization of words to vocalization of sound to nonvocal sound and back again, and in the violent, breathtaking transitions in and out of this chorus and indeed between all the perfectly integrated and overlapping fragments of this record.

What is that something? Damn if I know. But I know where you can find it.

First release: Brother 1001, July 1967

16

I Believe You Anyway
(*Good Vibrations, 30 Years of the Beach Boys*)

In 1993 I decided to start Crawdaddy! *again, specifically so I would have a place to write about music without the restrictions of length and style ("attitude") and marketplace consciousness that dominate all journalism. With no one to answer to but me I was able to give myself assignments like, "Listen to this five-CD Beach Boys 'box set' intensively for two solid months and then 'review' it, at any length you want. Write your heart out."* Okay, boss.

Life is imperfect. And so endlessly filled with blessings! In Lewis Shiner's new novel *Glimpses*, an alcoholic stereo repairman whose marriage is falling apart discovers he has a mysterious ability to imagine famous unfinished recordings in such detail that he and others can hear them and reproduce them as bootleg albums. He starts with a Beatles track and goes on to "trick" Jim Morrison into completing the Doors' *Celebration of the Lizard*, and then tackles the most legendary unreleased rock album of all time, the Beach Boys' *Smile*, with mixed results (immaculate babe born, world rejoices, mother lost in childbirth).

Meanwhile in the summer of 1993, coincident with the publication of *Glimpses*, Brian Wilson's legendary *Smile* recordings have finally arrived at your local record store after 26 years, not with a bang but a whisper.

They're part of a new box set (hey, every time you turn around there's a new box set; who even notices any more?)

called *Good Vibrations, 30 Years of the Beach Boys.* $60 is a lot of money, but my advice is, eat peanut butter for a month if you have to, the music will sustain you. Hog heaven, at least for this unrepentant Beach Boys lover: five compact discs, 141 tracks, more than six hours of music, and only two or three tracks in the whole shebang that don't make me grin at least a little bit. When I retired from *Crawdaddy!* the first time, end of 1968, and moved to a cabin in the woods in Mendocino, one of my dreams was that I'd systematically listen to the Beach Boys' entire catalog, immerse myself in it for months and come out with some kind of summing-up essay and a much deeper understanding of this beast called music and my heart relationship with it.

Never happened, and I'm not going to try to live out my childhood fantasies now. I think. But certainly one of the best aspects of the boxed set craze is the opportunity it gives us listeners to re-explore, in depth, a body of work that we've mostly experienced in album-sized chunks up to now. (Imagine a Who box set featuring all the singles from the '60s, properly mastered so they sound like they're played on a 45 rpm phonograph, if that's possible on CD, with the best B-sides and alternate takes and live fragments, plus "A Quick One" and "Rael" and the other genuine high points. Death to *Tommy* revivals!) Putting aside the sonic advantages (and occasional limitations) of CDs, there's no denying the useful-ness of being able to listen to so much music with so little effort. On the surface it may seem just a matter of convenience – but if, in 25 years, a passionate BBs fan like myself has never quite managed to surround himself with their music as thoroughly as he's always wanted to, until this box arrived, then I think we must acknowledge that form sometimes is almost as important as content in terms of what we actually do get around to experiencing.

(Turned my CDs into cassettes and listened to the entire six hours and 20 minutes in one sitting, driving the California interstate from San Francisco to San Diego. Wow. A hundred

126

or so years from now, when there are no cars or freeways any more, people will be spending their life savings for the opportunity to have such an experience.)

Life is imperfect, but something in us longs for perfection. *Pet Sounds* and "Good Vibrations" (album and single created by Brian Wilson in 1966 at the height of his powers; vocals by the Beach Boys) are as close to musical perfection as can be found in modern rock and roll or whatever you wanna call it, but Brian like Icarus saw a higher place to fly towards. Stunned by the beauty of the aforementioned discs, I found my way to Brian's mansion at Christmastime 1966, smoked grass with him inside the Arabian tent in his living room, listened to acetates of unbelievable, heavenly music from the *Smile* album in progress, attended a recording session, traded jokes and insights in the heated outdoor pool at four a.m., the lights of L.A. twinkling far beneath us, and eventually made my way back to New York to spread the word, like other journalists before and after me. Present at the creation of the myth.

The *Smile* album David Leaf, Mark Linett and Andy Paley have compiled for this box set (building on the efforts of Carl Wilson and others before them) is not perfect, of course; not the mythical beast he and we fantasized and promised. But – and it shocks me to be saying this, after all these years and all this hype – neither is it a disappointment. It's a tour de force, a thrilling, charming, revolutionary piece of work, obviously unfinished but still worthy to nestle beside *Pet Sounds* and the rest of the best of what contemporary musicians have accomplished. We weren't crazy after all. Listen to this. Listen.

The way to listen to the new "Child of *Smile*" album, I suggest, is to put Disc 2 of *Good Vibrations* on the CD player and start with track 18. Let it play to the end of the disc. Twelve tracks, 32 minutes of music. (About the length of a typical Beach Boys album from that era or any other, although *Smile* like *Pet Sounds* was conceived of as a more extended work.) Don't include "Good Vibrations," or the 45 rpm version of "Heroes and Villains" that opens Disc 3. Don't think about what did or didn't get included, or any other might-have-beens. Listen, over and over, like you listen to any record that lands in your hands: as a *fait accompli*. This is the album that is. Do you hear anything in it?

I hear a lot. Let me back up for a moment and say that this 32-minute *Smile* album, as exquisitely pleasurable and historically Significant as it is, does not overshadow the rest of this box. It's not a 600-pound canary. It fits in. This is a box full of astonishing, earthy, complex and simple-minded and gorgeously beautiful music. I don't always reach for Disc 2. I don't find myself dodging Disc 4, the one with the later, '70s and '80s, material. I enjoy the whole package (how many box sets can you say that about?). Disc 5, the "bonus" disc containing recordings of recording sessions and miscellaneous live performances and songs split so you can hear vocals without instruments or instrumental tracks without vocals, is the one I don't reach for quite as often – it contains some incredible treasures, but lacks the sweet flow of the other CDs. For particular occasions.

The box rises very successfully to an unusually difficult challenge: it has to satisfy two quite different constituencies of Beach Boys fans, who can be described roughly as those who might go see the band play live if they came through town, and those who bought copies of Brian Wilson's 1988 solo album. Messrs. Leaf, Linett and Paley have succeeded at this daunting task by arranging the songs on the four CDs in chronological order, packaging the fifth CD semi-separately as a "bonus bootleg disc," including all the BBs' top 40 hits up through 1988's surprise non-Brian hit "Kokomo," and at the same time including much of the long-awaited *Smile* material and a tremendous number of other unreleased recordings from throughout the Beach Boys' career. The rewards of the box set are substantial, in other words, whether one is inclined to view the Beach Boys as pure pop (nostalgic or newly-discovered – one testament to the quality of this music is how enthusiastically it is embraced by each new generation of subteens that encounters it, almost

128

regardless of cultural context) or as vital and remarkable semi-high art.

Lotsa good stuff. Disc 1 opens with a track that should delight both constituencies, even though its purely musical value is questionable: it's Brian Wilson's piano demo of "Surfin' USA," sung with tremendous heart and spirit in a flat, breaking, painfully raw voice. Brian was 20, and he had not yet sung lead on a Beach Boys single – "Surfin'" (11/61), "Surfin' Safari" (8/62, their first top 20 record), "409," and "Ten Little Indians" were all Mike Love leads, as was the released version of "Surfin' USA" (3/63 – the peculiar "30 years" in the box set title apparently refers to this single, because "it was their first top 10 hit"). Brian was shy. His idea of how to write a song in those days was: write an anthem about surfing (a nod to brother Dennis who first suggested the idea and perhaps made all this possible). He did it on the first two singles, the third flopped, now he'd thought of a way to do it again by writing new lyrics to Chuck Berry's "Sweet Little Sixteen" and his excitement is evident and infectious. (He would soon do it yet again on "Surf City," a song he wrote and gave to Jan & Dean, who made it a #1 hit.)

So where is Brian on this song? We hear Mike's voice on the final version, and Carl's charming Chuck Berry guitar riffs, we hear Berry's melody and arrangement, with words ostensibly written by Brian (most of them, he acknowledges, were a kind of found art in that he asked his girlfriend's brother to write down the names of all the good surfing spots he could think of). Brian is there in some of the flourishes ("inside outside USA"), but the demo calls attention to a deeper truth: he's there everywhere in the song, not because he produced it but because *he thought of it,* it's his vision, he pulled all the parts together out of his inspiration and enthusiasm and will. Musically this is expressed on the demo in the lilt of the sloppy vocal performance, the freshness and fierceness of the piano rhythm (actually a dumb/brilliant evolution of what Berry created, although the finished song sounds more like the

Berry version), and most of all in the unearthly beauty of the brief falsetto parts, "Everybody's gone surfin' . . ." This is the essence of the matter. This is what those of us who've fallen in love with this music listen for, I suggest. I call it a mysterious spirituality, because of the effect it has on me. Cindy speaks of an irresistible sadness in the voice. Whatever it is, it's there in that falsetto, not the product of genius in the sense of some kind of studio mastery or compositional talent but rather a direct, crude gift for the expression of feeling through voice, music, melody. "Everybody's gone surfin' . . ." A very psychedelic moment. This man knows something (whether he admits it to himself or not). Like all great American singers and music makers, he has seen (heard, felt) the glory.

Disc 1, which takes us to the beginning of 1965, is roughly the equivalent of the excellent 1974 compilation *Endless Summer*: it sums up the early, surf (cars, fun) era of the Beach Boys. (It does offer quite a few tracks that aren't on *Endless Summer*, including such gems as "Don't Back Down," "Please Let Me Wonder," "When I Grow Up (to Be a Man)" and "Why Do Fools Fall in Love?") I know there are people who regard *Pet Sounds* as the greatest album of all time who don't appreciate the Beach Boys' earlier recordings, but such a position is indefensible, probably the result of cultural prejudice. It (music, art) doesn't get any better than "Don't Worry Baby," "I Get Around," "The Warmth of the Sun," or "Fun, Fun, Fun." The musical ideas, groundbreaking then, are still full of revelation today. The sonic beauty of the recordings is unsurpassed. This is the rock and roll aesthetic, compressing the meaning of existence (and all the feelings such contemplation, conscious and unconscious, stirs up in us) into a two-minute performance, totally present and in your face and just as suddenly gone again, except for certain melodic or verbal or rhythmic hooks left behind. What was that? Play it again. Re-experience it. Drink it in. Still full of all those stirred up feelings, but no longer alone with them.

(One caveat. I would like to believe that sonic perfection is forever, but in fact it's as much a will-o'-the-wisp as the rest of our supermodern reality. Mark Linett has done a superb job massaging these tracks into digital CD-encoded form, but this whole milieu of ephemeral hardware that allows and requires endless remastering of earlier recordings is treacherous. No one can really say how these recordings should sound, except possibly Brian Wilson, and if able he's certainly not willing to direct the proceedings. The problem is, when we're talking about magical sounds, relationships are everything. I believe the oooooweeees at the end of "Fun, Fun, Fun" are the defining moment of the record (bookending and trumping the perfect son-of-JBG guitar intro). But in my mind and memory they should soar free, dominating the record's fade while everything else slips to the background, not swamped into the chorus like one more special effect. The song *is* that triumphant falsetto swoop, and to my ears it's lost here, at least on the various CD players I've tried it on – a very great loss indeed. I know that if I go back and listen to a variety of earlier cassette and vinyl copies of the song, what I'm wanting to hear may be elusive there as well, depending on the pressing and other factors, notably the nature of the equipment I'm listening on (one phonograph's not the same as another, by a long shot). And the kind of 1960s AM radio top 40 transmission and compression that these singles were designed for simply does not exist any more at all, no more than the car and transistor radios that received the signals. Lost in time. Anyway, I guess I'm acknowledging that there is no objective truth in such matters, but still I feel certain that if I were standing next to the sound engineer with a bomb in my hand this CD version of "Fun, Fun, Fun" could sound a lot closer to a certain subjective ideal I happen to feel rather strongly about.)

I like the guitar sound on "Surfin' Safari." I like the haunting melody of the 20-second unfinished fragment called "Little Surfer Girl." I have always loved "Shut Down" and "In My Room" and still do – the former appealed to me when I didn't even like rock and roll, and I certainly wasn't into cars or drag racing, but there was something about the unique sound and structure of the song, that *tautness*, never heard anything like it. As for "In My Room," I guess I'm a sucker for Brian's terrifyingly honest confessions and expressions of feelings most folks never even talk about ("Don't Worry Baby," "In the Back of My Mind," "Please Let Me Wonder"). That is the key to *Pet Sounds*, just as much as the extraordinary arrangements and melodies. I'd even argue that the quality of Brian's melodies is also due to a kind of honesty. And courage. I love the vocal, the harmonies, the hypnotic pace of the thing, the high "oo" in the middle of "room" at the end of the track . . . And oh yeah, I've always been fascinated by the lyrical and philosophical similarities between "In My Room" and the Beatles' "There's a Place," recorded six months earlier but how likely is it that Brian or Gary Usher imported the album from England? "There's a place/world where I can go . . ." John's was his mind, Brian's his room, and there you have it, sports fans.

I like "The Surfer Moon" 'cause I never really listened to it before. "Catch a Wave" is a gem I'd overlooked or underrated (layers of sound!). Crank it up. "Don't Back Down" a shining example of Brian at his best I hadn't really connected with till now. Or I did, and forgot, and this box is the occasion of a happy reunion and rediscovery.

And more. Fascinating to listen to "Surfer Girl" and realize Brian wrote it at the same time as or before "Surfin'," the very beginning. How it contains the essence of all that was to come later. Recorded it again and released it as a single with his own lead vocal just as soon as he got his Dad and the Capitol guys out of the studio, their first ballad single, and second top ten hit. Those harmonies. He may have been thrilled and inspired by the Four Freshmen, but this is something different. His own little discovery/invention. A vision of harmony. How we (each appreciated for his own special qualities) could be together.

And lots more stuff. Fount of creativity. Listen. Listen. Listen.

The imperfection in Disc 2 is simple (and unavoidable): listening to selections from *Pet Sounds* is like listening to an edited version of your favorite song. Eight *Pet Sounds* songs are included here, and it's either too many or not enough. Immediately and every time I find myself missing the other five songs: the astonishing and underrated "Here Today," "Don't Talk (Put Your Head on My Shoulder)" (some days my favorite Brian Wilson song), "Let's Go Away for Awhile," "I'm Waiting for the Day," and "That's Not Me." The compilers have a seeming prejudice against Mike Love lead vocals, which I don't share. Mike's leads on "Here Today" and "Sloop John B" and "I Know There's an Answer" are an important part of the magic of *Pet Sounds* – much as I love Brian's vocals, the sound of the album would be thinner and a lot less perfect without Mike's voice. Along the same lines, it's wonderful to be able to hear Brian's draft vocal for "God Only Knows" (included with other pieces of the session on Disc 5), but gorgeous as it is it can't touch the finished version and Carl's extraordinary vocal performance. The point is that Brian is a painter, and the sound of the Beach Boys' voices is the most important part of his palette. His process is not precisely to create sounds, but to find them and put them together. At the time of *Pet Sounds*, even though he was making something that could easily have been called a solo album, he was at the peak of his creative powers partly because he still had complete and un-self-conscious access to the palette of sounds, vocal and instrumental, that he had worked with over the years, along with all the new sounds he was discovering and uncovering every time he walked into the studio.

Anyway, I'm not saying the compilers should have done it differently. But the real Beach Boys box set is the one you have here plus the *Pet Sounds* CD (exquisitely mastered by Mark Linett). Some things can't be excerpted.

Disc 2 starts with two of the Beach Boys' biggest hits, "California Girls" and "Help Me, Rhonda." Both songs have always bugged me – they get old for me much faster (I get tired of hearing them) than most of the Beach Boys' oeuvre. I'm not sure why this is. I don't care much for the lead vocals on either song (Mike on "California Girls," Alan on "Help Me, Rhonda"), and the lyrics of "California Girls" are irritating for their cuteness as well as their double chauvinism. But I think there's an irritation factor in the music as well, by which I guess I mean the arrangement of both songs. Is it possible that Brian the eternal innocent is displaying a bit of cynicism here? He does come up with some fresh musical ideas in these songs (I wish the compilers had put the two songs in their proper chronological order, instead of yielding to the temptation to put the eternally popular "California Girls" at the start of the disc), but finally there's a shallowness for me, a slickness, maybe an absence of that mysterious spiritual quality that's present even in songs like "Wendy" and "The Girls on the Beach." I don't know. I do like the long keyboard intro to "California Girls," and I notice that the chorus of the song introduces the "round" effect that is used so well on *Pet Sounds*. But I can't feel the warmth of the sun in either of these songs, or not as strong as I want to feel it. Brian's salute to Phil Spector, "Then I Kissed Her" (sung by Al again, a Beach Boy who seldom sings lead), is fun but nothing special. What I really like amidst this strange miscellany (Brian seems to have been floundering about a bit in '65, trying on different styles, looking for something and tossing off records – always under pressure from Capitol and others to produce, make us some more money kid – the way other people write postcards) is the one-minute a cappella snippet "And Your Dream Comes True," and the playful, atavistic "Barbara Ann." Pure essence of Brian, even if there's no studio whiz kid anywhere in evidence.

The transition into *Pet Sounds*, on the box set and as a matter of historical fact, is another odd experiment, a cover of a folk song previously popularized by the Kingston Trio, "Sloop John B." At Al's suggestion, Brian recorded an instrumental track for this song in summer 1965, while "Help Me, Rhonda" and "California Girls" were dominating the charts and before he and the group made *Beach Boys Party!* in response to record company pressure (their third album of new material that year). In October "The Little Girl I Once Knew" was recorded (need a single!), in November the instrumentals "Pet Sounds" and "Trombone Dixie" (outtake included on the *Pet Sounds* CD) were laid down, and then just before Christmas Brian brought the group in to do vocals for "Sloop John B." Two other events are significant for this chronology: sometime in 1965 Brian took LSD for the first time, and was profoundly moved by the experience; and in late autumn the Beatles released a record called *Rubber Soul* that threw down the gauntlet as far as what a rock and roll *album* could be. Brian like the Beatles had previously thought of his work in terms of single songs, but he was ready and eager to rise to the challenge.

"The Little Girl I Once Knew" is an inventive recording, but certainly not an ambitious one. "Pet Sounds," the instrumental, is very ambitious: you can hear the arranger/ composer/producer trying hard to capture something, a sound he hears in his head, a feeling, a whole set of sounds and feelings. "Sloop John B," reportedly only on the album because the record company insisted (but an integral part of it nonetheless through the miracle of *fait accompli*), splits the difference, a routine instrumental track with a delightful opening, but something happens to the vocals at the end of the first chorus and through the second verse and chorus that is transcendent. A door has been opened, and love and beauty and musical magic are flooding in. Specifically I'm talking about the dumb angelic "doot-doot" back-up vocal that starts after "I wanna go home," quickly joined by a wonderful density of sound, ooohs and bells and a soaring feeling of musical intensity and momentum, that patented Brian Wilson

135

"saturate the track with music" effect, building up and bursting into the climactic a cappella "let me go home/hoist up the John B sails" vocal break in the second half of the second chorus, just amazing. Brian was ready. He wrote and recorded the rest of *Pet Sounds* between January and April of 1966.

So even as we're sitting here, someone is listening to the box set, her parents' copy, or he got it for his birthday, and hearing "God Only Knows" for the first time, really hearing it. And nothing will ever be the same again. Wow. Even after all these years and all the hype, I find the power of this art form awesome to contemplate. How does it do that? Why does music mean so much to people?

I have spent my life trying to answer this question, and still I don't know where to begin. What happens when I hear "God Only Knows"? I get feelings. Deep feelings. This matters because these feelings don't pass unnoticed. They have an impact. They bring about some kind of awakening, or a renewal, rediscovery, of faith. A sense of my own existence.

This is not achieved by anything that could be called "meaning." It's not about the meaning of the song. Nor is it about its musical innovations. It's about what it says, through its sound its performance its totality its presence, to our hearts.

Pleasure is an important part of it. Good music brings pleasure, like good sex with someone you love, or a walk in the woods. My pleasure in "God Only Knows" begins with the first note, the sound of it, the ways it makes me feel, the way it comes full blown out of nowhere, the melody that already seems implied in this first note or chord (I guess it's a bunch of notes at once), its personality, its intelligence, its warmth. Then the intro that follows, the orchestral sound (I could never guess what combination of instruments this is, but I love the feel of it, like the texture of a piece of rare cloth), the rhythm that's immediately established, the moment when the bass comes in and the sweetness of that bass line and the moment when the other instruments drop out. I could just listen to these 17 seconds over and over, like a cat lying in the sun. And then the heightened pleasure of the 18th second when the voice comes in, that transition, the purity and the beauty of the singing, the way the music and voice go together, the connection felt with another human being (music is spirit that becomes flesh when it's vocalized; hey that's a person, like me, I have a voice too), the way the melody he's singing keeps ascending, moving upward, and the power of *this* voice and *this* melodic progression speaking/sending these words:

> I may not always love you
> But long as there are stars above you
> You'll never need to doubt it
> I'll make you so sure about it
> God only knows what I'd be without you . . .

I don't want to say any more, except to acknowledge that I'm just as excited and fulfilled by the other verses, and the amazing little musical transitions between them, and the instrumental/vocal bridge in the middle of the song, oh and most of all the ending of the song, the repeating ascending round of individual voices, one atop the other in an ecstatic loop, the most heavenly 47 seconds in contemporary music. What does it arouse in me? I feel accepted. I feel forgiven. I feel called, and better yet, I feel the energy and the will and the self-confidence to answer. Inspiration. I feel full of the breath of life.

Hey, it's just a song. Yeah. Wind me up and I can wax just as enthusiastic about "You Still Believe in Me." And "I Just Wasn't Made for These Times." And *Pet Sounds* as a whole. The sound of Brian's voice, of all the voices, of those incredible live in-studio orchestras (no instrumental overdubs!). David Leaf's liner notes (in the box set, and the more detailed notes he wrote for the *Pet Sounds* CD) provide a great deal of fascinating information about how the album was recorded. But all you need is ears. And an open heart. There's no other album like this one.

But Brian couldn't help trying to top himself anyway.

137

"Good Vibrations" is a record I don't get tired of. I screen it out sometimes, deal with its omnipresence by ignoring it or taking it for granted, but whenever I do choose to give it my attention I *always* find myself richly rewarded. Most spectacular collection of transitions in rock and roll history (take that, Mr. Spector). This is the three-and-a-half-minute symphony every marijuana-dazed '60s rocker dreamed of recording, and no one else really came close. Some kind of miracle. The sound of those voices! No way it would sound half as good if all the parts were sung by Brian. Real genius is more than conceptual. It gets its hands dirty. It shapes deathless sculptures out of clay found in the artist's backyard.

"Good Vibrations" took six months to record (April-September 1966) and huge quantities of money and studio time, but there are indications that this had more to do with self-consciousness than creative necessity. The engineer on the project feels that Brian had 90% of the song the first time he recorded it, and that the lengthy and complex process he went through in the months that followed ultimately served to bring him back to something very close to his original inspiration.

"Good Vibrations" began during the *Pet Sounds* recording sessions, but Brian correctly (intuitively) perceived that it was not meant for that album, that it had a different flavor and character and required a different approach. It was his greatest juggling act, see how many balls I can keep in the air without losing the great-hearted vulnerability of spirit that makes my music worth listening to. He did it. And then . . .

The *Smile* album that's been cobbled together for inclusion in this box set, 26 years after the fact, starts with a timeless a cappella invocation (stark and soothing and startlingly beautiful) called "Our Prayer." It's a wonderful wordless beginning for a record that for the most part uses words the same way it uses strings and keyboards – for their sounds. This is in sharp contrast to *Pet Sounds*, where most of the songs have titles and lyrics that evoke specific situations and feelings. *Smile*'s radicalism begins with and centers around the fact that it is

138

abstract, whereas all previous Beach Boys records and most rock and roll songs are concrete in their imagery. They have words, and those words generally tell a story. Van Dyke Parks' impressionistic *Smile* lyrics resist literal comprehension, but I think it would be a mistake to think it was Van who led Brian down this bold and risky path of abstract expression. Rather, Brian chose Van Dyke as a writing partner because his peculiar (and magical) way with words and ideas and images seemed perfectly suited to the vision that had already powerfully seized Brian's imagination. (Earlier in the year, I suggest, Brian chose Tony Asher as a collaborator because he needed someone square and articulate; now he grabbed Van Dyke Parks because he needed a co-writer who was, so to speak, inarticulate, and hip.)

The primary abstractions on *Smile* are not lyrical but musical. This is evident as the second track on the album ("Heroes and Villains," unreleased version) spills over into the third track, "Heroes and Villains (Sections)." The "Sections" track is six minutes and 40 seconds of pleasing, intelligent, highly experimental music, with an important couplet at the beginning ("Bicycle rider, just see what you've done/Done to the church of the American Indian") and then no other identifiable words except "heroes and villains" and once, delightfully – climax to an out-of-nowhere doo-wop chorus – "how I love my girl!"

Brian in 1964 when he wrote "Don't Worry Baby" (with help from Roger Christian) was, mostly unconsciously, breaking through the limits of language, so that a song about a teenager challenged to a drag race became something hugely more immediate (and unspeakable) for both singer and listener. Now he wants to break through the limits of language consciously, wants to apply to his new album not only what he's learned from "Good Vibrations," but also what he's learned from "Barbara Ann." The communicative power of the human voice singing, for example, "Ba- Ba- Ba-, Ba- Barbara Ann." What is that? "Everybody's gone *surf*in' . . ." Those ooohs. He's

139

built a career on those ooohs. Knows they touch people, knows how to touch people with them, feels fulfilled when the connection is made. Brian like any great performer/producer has always spoken in tongues, "imitations of speech" more powerful than speech itself. Now he wants to speak in tongues more openly, less hiding behind narratives, no surf anthems, no teenage love songs or even cool songs of existential angst. Just, um, sounds that I like. Tripped-out sounds that I like. In the form of music, of course. Rhythmic, melodic, stimulating, seductive, reassuring music. With trippy funny important (relevant) stories and images encoded in the lyrics and/or in the choice of vocal and instrumental material. (It seems fair to say, listening to these tracks, that Brian Wilson was one of the earliest pioneers of sampling.) Hey. Listen to this.

Does it work? Gotta kill history to get an honest or fair answer to this question. Forget the drama, forget the expectations, forget if you can the context of all this, forget even that this work is unfinished and that its creator has not actively participated in its preparation for release. Forget that there's another "Heroes and Villains" (which happens to be one of my favorite records of all time). Forget the confusion created by the bandying about of that meaningless word "genius." Listen naked. And listen and listen. Are you getting into the rhythm, the sense, the feel of the album? Is it taking on a form of its own? Do you like it?

I do. Very much. But because of the way the album has been built up over the years, I feel a need to point out that you should not feel dumb if you don't enjoy it. It's not a work of genius. (*Pet Sounds* probably is, but that's another story.) It's a passionate experiment that both succeeds and fails. As a failure, it's famous. Its success, now that we all can hear it, is likely to be much more modest. But these words of mine are mixing up artistic success and public recognition. In hindsight, it may in fact have been impossible for Brian, even under the best of circumstances, to pull together *Smile* the way he envisioned it. There's no way to know. It's easy to imagine

140

that the man who could pull together "Good Vibrations" could pull together anything. Maybe. Anyway, he didn't do it, and maybe in fact there was no way to take all these endless excellent snippets and alternate sections of "Heroes and Villains" and many other songs and merge them together into a single unified work of music that would provoke immediate recognition and pleasure in its listeners the way all Brian's songs (and his one great album) had done until now.

But we have the sessions. And the best or most coherent of those sessions, more or less, have been assembled here and released to the public, in an arbitrary but well-thought-out and highly gratifying (sez me) sequence. Child of *Smile*. I've been listening to it a lot. And it amazes me.

Putting aside the myth (which David Anderle and I certainly helped create, in our published conversation way back a long time ago) of the genius artist frustrated on the brink of his greatest masterwork, these tracks are clearly the work of someone very stoned, a powerful creative artist very much under the influence of marijuana and amphetamines. He was also stoned on power, the power of having the money and the reputation, the intelligence and the talent and the fear/respect of the people around you, that allows you to do whatever you feel like, whatever you think of. Amphetamine makes the user imagine he has such power; in Brian's case, at that moment, he really did have it (almost). Look out world.

And of course the people around him, the witnesses to his "genius," David Anderle, Van Dyke Parks, Derek Taylor, the journalists like myself, were also very stoned. This could possibly have had some effect on our assessment of what was going on.

I don't mean to sound cynical. History is subjective, and I just want to take this opportunity to remind you of the subjectivity of the historians. Brian Wilson is an artist whose achievements are truly substantial (as evidenced by the box set); but for 26 years now he has been judged not on his achievement but on his potential. This is unfair and misleading. *Pet Sounds* is one of the greatest albums of our era. Why should it be eclipsed by the "even greater album" that turned out to be a pipe dream?

Being stoned definitely promotes original and unusual ideas in creative people, and it also serves to make one less inhibited about exploring and using those ideas. This is genuine, this is a plus. On the minus side, being stoned often makes dumb ideas seem terrific; it makes you laugh at things other people wouldn't see the humor in (not a problem unless you've decided to record an album that includes "lots of humor"); and while (especially fueled by amphetamines) it gives you plenty of energy to start things, it very often leaves you without the energy to finish them. A more subtle aspect of being high on marijuana or hashish that many people have noticed is that it stimulates the "head" (mental ideas) but suppresses the heart, the responsive, "feeling-based" side of the personality.

There are moments of great sensitivity and deep feeling on these *Smile* tracks (notably Brian's vocal performances on "Wonderful" and "Surf's Up"), but in its overall character it is not at all a "heart" album (as *Pet Sounds* certainly is); rather it is, and was clearly meant to be, a sort of three-ring circus of flashy musical ideas and avant-garde entertainment. Many of the tracks contain brief segments of truly extraordinary beauty and musical originality (it was hearing some of these tracks, as acetates, that got me and other visitors so excited). The presumption that Brian was working on a masterpiece and would pull it off was based on the obvious ambitiousness and fecundity of the work in progress, and on the astonishing model of "Good Vibrations," which seemed to prove that in the end Brian could take all these fragments and miraculously sew them together into a whole even greater than the sum of its parts. Maybe. Maybe not. Ironically, I think the 45-rpm version of "Heroes and Villains" that Brian put together with fresh vocals near the end of the *Smile* period, which has been criticized as an abandonment of the *Smile* vision, is the best

142

example other than "Good Vibrations" of Brian's ability to unify a thousand working drafts into a brief, coherent, magnificently heartfelt finished statement. But by creating an actuality, we put an end to all the fantasized possibilities. The moral is: don't let anyone watch you paint. They'll always feel (and sometimes be brash enough to say) that the canvas they thought they saw emerging halfway through was oh so much more beautiful.

("You never knew what I loved in you; I don't know what you loved in me/Maybe the picture of somebody you were hoping I might be." – Jackson Browne, "Late for the Sky")

Goodbye, sweet genius. Could we have the hard-working guy back now, please?

What *Smile* has, instead of the radical but intuitively ear-pleasing structure and irresistible spirit of celebration found in "Good Vibrations" and "I Get Around," and instead of the unearthly beauty and oh-so-human emotional nakedness of "The Warmth of the Sun" and *Pet Sounds*, is an enthusiasm for life (what I saw when I came out of my room, and before I got scared again) and a love of music in all its possible forms, a love of the human voice in all its myriad manifestations, a fascination with the relationship between music and voice, and a veritable eruption of musical and sonic insights, new language, new combinations. It compresses half a dozen different songs into one ("Cabinessence"), and at the same time it repeats a single melodic and rhythmic theme (the "Heroes and Villains" chorus) in otherwise separate songs, breaking down the walls that give songs identities without ever offering conceptual ("rock opera") explanation or resolution. It is a series of visions, some muddied but tantalizing, others breathtakingly clear and full of a beauty that is itself the pure product of wonder. *Smile* has sense of wonder. Beyond humor, it expresses awe at the entire human and natural universe, and reaches out unselfconsciously to capture the sound of that awe and amusement in music and voice. It sparkles.

143

It is also perhaps the story of the unnatural love affair between one man's voice and a harpsichord.

"Heroes and Villains" runs everywhere and remains elusive. David Leaf tells us plainly (in the liner notes to the reissue of *Smiley Smile*) that the original eleven-minute single that Brian almost released in January 1967 has yet to be found, that if it had been located it would have been included on that reissue, and this one. And there's lots more "Heroes and Villains" lying around. But there's also this confusion as to where one song starts or stops. "Do You Like Worms" was a separate enough song-idea to be included on the jacket Capitol printed for the ill-fated album, and yet the track included here is full of "Heroes and Villains" choruses, along with the wonderful "Plymouth Rock roll over" refrain (nothing about worms). Who's zooming who? "Vegetables" has a strong tune and verse identity all its own, but it's at its best between verses (and in the long coda at the end) when it bursts into pure *Smile* vocalizations, manifestations of a higher reality, unmistakably music that belongs to the album as a whole rather than to any one song.

I love the two discrete, narrative (verging on the abstract or even the fractal, but still distinctly narrative) songs Van Dyke and Brian managed to write together, "Wonderful" and "Surf's Up." I am amazed at the beauty and grace of "Wonderful," "Wind Chimes" and "Vegetables" in contrast to the awkward raw goofiness of the *Smiley Smile* versions. I like "Cabinessence" even better in the supportive company of these other perform- ances than I did when it was first released (on *20/20* in 1969). I am pleased and tantalized by the "words" version of "Heroes and Villains" here, very visual narrative like the start of a film that then trails off as though the words have either been forgotten or the camera's pulled so far back you can't hear them, like the whole album's the continuation of the narra- tive. Listen. I love not most of all but equally with "H&V" (verbal) and "Wonderful" and "Surf's Up" the nonverbal vocal/instrumental presence that weaves its way throughout

144

the album, overtly on "Our Prayer" and "H&V (Sections)" and "H & V Intro" and "Do You Like Worms" and "I Love to Say Da Da" (and on "With Me Tonight" if you include that on your *Smile* album; I do because I like it a lot and because it's there, fait accompli, I don't want to jump up and stop the CD just because I know it was actually recorded a couple of months later), and covertly absolutely everywhere, I mean the nonverbal embraces and almost swallows the verbal even in such delicately articulate and word-centered moments as "a boy bumped into her" and "canvas the town and brush the backdrop."

There is no other album like this, no music like this. "Wa wa ho wa." Myths die hard in Auld Lang Syne but – come about hard, already, okay? Find your way in, dear listener. You're going to truly delight in this record.

So: after a Disc 1 which contains most of the great early singles that made the Beach Boys famous and which speak so immediately and pleasurably to all innocent listeners in any era, and a Disc 2 which contains "Good Vibrations" and much of *Pet Sounds* and the first release of the legendary *Smile,* what's left? Why it's the third era of the Beach Boys, the secret era, the not-popular, not-legendary era that encompasses their last four Capitol/Brother albums and their first two for Warner Brothers, 1967–1971, a time when Brian and his brothers and extended family quietly and awkwardly produced some of their most enduring and most endearing music. At the big science fiction gathering I attended this past weekend I met a number of people who have been listening to this box set as hungrily and happily and perpetually as I have, and several of them volunteered that Disc 3 is their favorite, the one they find themselves drawn to most often and insistently. Me too. I love Disc 3. The post-ambitious period. Here as much as anywhere is the real genius of Brian Wilson, the real achievement of Brian and the Beach Boys. Here as much as anywhere is the music for which they will be remembered well into the next century.

145

First of all, of course, here is "Heroes and Villains," the original single, which I have already described here and in my book *The 100 Best Singles* as one of my most beloved records of all time. In a sense Brian went back into the studio and recorded all of *Smile* in three and a half minutes. This truly is genius, and it went unappreciated in its time and still today, as people waited for something more obvious and pretentious (and they got it, too, in the form of *Sgt. Pepper*). If there was indeed a conscious creative genius somewhere inside Brian, I think it withdrew in a pout when this single went unheralded, silent with the egotistic fury usually associated with French chefs, vowing never again to cast its pearls before such swine. Harrumph. Well, that's the pop music biz. Live by the sword of mass popularity (and critical worship) and you'll die by the sword. It's still an inexpressibly beautiful piece of music.

And there are at least two other recordings on Disc 3 worthy of mention in the same breath, two other masterpieces worth the price of the box set all by their lonesome selves: "Can't Wait Too Long" (1967/1968) and the reworked "Surf's Up" (1966/1971).

"Can't Wait Too Long" is a delicious surprise. It first surfaced a few years ago as a bonus track on the CD "twofer" of *Smiley Smile* and *Wild Honey*. The box set version is an alternate edit and mix, and while the first version is a splendid find ("the single best piece of unreleased music in the Beach Boys archive," David Leaf wrote in 1990), this new version is hugely better, thanks to a welcome abbreviation of the repeating chorus in the middle (eight repetitions instead of sixteen; works much better) and a different mix that reveals the spoken/sung section just before those repetitions, a brief, possibly accidental segment that gives me gooseflesh and unending pleasure equal to the closing movement of "God Only Knows" or my favorite Bob Dylan performances. I must say, however, that comparison of the two versions requires me to mention another of the very few flaws in this box set: the last 40 seconds of "Can't Wait Too Long," a bass-driven

146

instrumental break reminiscent of "Shortening Bread," is inexplicably missing from version two, and the song is the poorer for it (instead we get a clever, but frustrating, segue into "Cool, Cool Water"). In other words, for the perfect "Can't Wait Too Long" one must tape the box set version and then add the ending from version one. A regrettable error. But it embarrasses me to be even slightly critical of the gentlemen who are responsible for the fact that we have this exquisite bit of "unfinished" music in the first place.

"Can't Wait Too Long" is truly mysterious in both its complexity and its simplicity. Like "Good Vibrations," like "Heroes and Villains," it's one of a kind; there really is no other piece of music quite like it. The man who later in 1968 would put out an album entitled *Stack-o-Tracks* seems to have been dreaming on tape here, stacking up instrumental and background vocal tracks into a snippet of music entirely outside of normal song structure, yet as certifiably ear candy (listener-friendly) as any of Brian's early pop creations . . . and for all its ethereal abstractness the song has a brilliant and haunting lyric of extraordinary cleverness, as "been way too long" slips into "can't wait too long" and back again. The opening line, "I miss you darling, I miss you so hard" is also a striking bit of language, especially as sung here, and along with the earlier choral fragment "Been . . . so . . . long" it easily carries an opening minute and 42 seconds in which these are the only words. There is no way of knowing now whether this gloriously successful use of a few words to flavor and give emotional specificity to a long, complex, deeply express-ive nonverbal passage (remember that with Brian nonverbal doesn't mean nonvocal; when background vocals become part of the foreground like this, what shall we call them?) is inten-tional or simply an example of a track for which lead vocals were planned but not completed.

The mystery deepens, and the power and beauty of the song increase almost unbearably, in the next 23 seconds, as Carl sings again "Miss you darling, I miss you so hard" and Brian,

speaking, echoes "miss you so hard" and seems to be teaching
Carl (and others?) the rest of the words while the track is
playing. He says/sings: "Now, 'Come back baby and don't
break my heart.' " The idea that this is an instructional or
guide vocal is my assumption, and may be all wrong, but in any
case the musicality of Brian's (it is Brian, isn't it?) spoken
phrase, the way it leans into each beat of the track, is magical,
and if the effect were consciously planned would certainly
be deserving of the G word. I believe Brian then mutters,
"And it goes (break)" – and we hear this sparkling keyboard
sound and a heartstoppingly beautiful bit of speaksinging:
"And now I'm alone lying down looking up at the stars" (Carl
echoes, adding melody and more heart, "stars") "Reliving the"
(melodic fragment from Brian I think, as a reference, then
right back to speaking without missing a beat) "Reliving the
times we shared with the moon and stars and the music we
love," split-second breath and then I'm guessing it's Brian
and Carl singing together live but who knows, anyway a classic majestic Brian transition into "Been way too long, been
way too long baby . . ." Wow. That moment, that two-line epic
poem of Brian's about lying down looking up at the stars,
reliving the times we shared, is a complete stoppage of time,
quick trip to eternity. Sexual love and the Grand Canyon
and modern computer technology are wondrous things but
no more awesome than this fragment of music, what is that,
where did it come from, how did it get here? What are these
feelings it evokes in me? Whew. I won't walk you through the
rest of the track, but it's not a letdown. Some kind of place
where conscious genius and accidental, spontaneous genius
meet . . . and the track we're left with is like a photograph
someone took who happened to be standing there at that
magic moment.

  "Surf's Up" is another kind of magic; in its finished form it's
a masterful nostalgic evocation by Carl of a time gone by, that
moment when Brian like Dennis before him ran into the
(musical) surf, full of excitement and wonder and a youthful

sense of immortality, hanging ten all smiles on the crest of a
tidal wave . . . I believe Van Dyke and Brian wrote this in an
evening, the day they first got together; if it's not true it's
mythologically appropriate anyway, pure collaboration, Brian
inspired by God and Van Dyke inspired by the divine melody
and rhythm and presence coming through Brian's fingertips
and vocalizations, and out spilled these punning word-sounds
so exquisitely evocative not just of the communal fantasies and
promises of 1966 in LSD-enhanced California/America but of
that moment in any person's or generation's life when the
power and promise of the future seems to open up before us
without limits, so that even sadder-but-wiser (actually very *fin-
de-siècle*) lyrics are experienced as that delicious pre-dawn sadness, part of the awakening, a farewell toast to the old world
(blind class aristocracy, columnated ruins) and also perhaps
smug youthful celebration of our own wisdom, our ability to
see the grand sweep of the past and (implicitly) the future. Am
I babbling? This song does that to me, reduces me to pure
feelings with millions of specific images loosely attached, floating by, all contradictory and all true at the moment that I see
and feel them.

The box set contains Brian's complete rough vocal with
piano from 1966 (Disc 2, *Smile* section) and the instrumental
track from 1966 (Disc 5) that Carl sings to in the first part
of the 1971 version (Brian '66 takes over with "Dove-nested
towers"). So we get the pieces of the puzzle (except the *Smile*
section doesn't offer the original "Child Is Father to the Man"
track that Carl et al. brilliantly reworked as the ecstatic conclusion to "Surf's Up"), but of course the whole is more than the
sum of its parts. There is a grace to the finished "Surf's Up"
that is positively otherworldly. When Brian's held note on
"song" explodes into the group singing "the child, the child,
the child" it is for me one of the happiest moments in contemporary music – and even so it's not my favorite among
this wonderful compilation of amazing transitions. That honor
belongs to the moment when Brian sings the words "Surf's up!

149

(mm mm)", and why does it move me so much more deeply in the later version when it's the exact same track? It must have to do with the greater piquancy Brian's vulnerable solo vocal takes on in the context of the fancy wild inventive music on the opening track and the patented "Beach Boys" feel of Carl's opening vocals – universal, collective, omnipresent. That "Surf's up!" moment, then, is not just a transition from what Brian was singing in the previous verse but rather a pivot on which everything that's come before in the song wheels and turns, and maybe not just everything that's in the song but everything the Beach Boys and Brian have sung and played and done up to this moment. The lyrics overtly refer to the Beach Boys' musical legacy at this point, indeed although it's Brian singing we can hear Van Dyke speaking *to* him, with love and compassion ("come about hard and join the young and often spring you gave"), more so even in hindsight than could possibly have been true when the lyrics were written. Mysterious (I said that before) the workings of songs and lyrics and performance. Magical (another much-used word) the impact all this has on us the listeners, moving far beyond the conscious and unconscious intentions of composers and performers (and after-the-fact assemblers) and into the private realm of our own feelings and personal histories. Singing to me. He's singing to me. And with tears in my eyes I thank him.

But carrying on about these three masterpieces only scratches the surface of what Disc 3 has to offer. "Darling" sounds better every year, wow. "Break Away" is a long-lost favorite I can't get enough of. *Friends* and *Wild Honey* and *Smiley Smile* and *20/20* all deserve to be listened to over and over in their entirety (so get the twofers), but the selections chosen here are intelligent and so pleasing, Dennis's "Little Bird," "I Went to Sleep," "Let the Wind Blow," "Time to Get Alone," "Do It Again," and the sublime fragment "Meant for You." "This Whole World" from *Sunflower.* " 'Til I Die" from *Surf's Up.* And some top-of-the-line unreleased tracks: "Games Two Can Play" (Brian, where do you get these melodies? How do you speak so directly and un-self-consciously?), "San Miguel" (Dennis again, why didn't he write more?), and the 1967 version of "Cool, Cool Water." These are not lesser works. The third era of the Beach Boys is every bit as rewarding as the first two. Brian gave up his crown but could not (yet) escape from his talent. The more time passes, and the further we get from the commercial and critical expectations placed on the Beach Boys at the time, the better this music sounds. What a triumph, how American, how Emersonian, to be able to be so disconnected from what's hip, what sells, what's fashionable. It's true, sadly true, that if it were not for what went before, no record company would ever have released any of these albums. Are there other Brian Wilsons out there, then, who never had a string of hits and whose idiosyncratic creations, however brilliant, are therefore unreleased and ignored? Maybe. Probably. But right now that's not the question. Instead we celebrate the accident or grace of God that has brought us wacky delights like "I Went to Sleep" and "Busy Doing Nothin'," and we listen not just with pleasure but fascination to the melodic, chromatic, harmonic, structural insights and innovations hidden within these seemingly simplistic creations.

Melodies. You'd think that there were only a handful of melodies in the world, especially given the way folk and country and rock and pop and jazz musicians continually borrow and recycle them, and then you listen to Brian Wilson, and can't stop listening, and wake up in the morning with the tune of "Games Two Can Play" or "Break Away" playing in your mind, irrepressible, and you have to think that here's a guy who's tapped into some larger musical universe. And you can complain about his problems and his laziness and the people who've exploited him and what we've lost perhaps, but who among us can say they've come anywhere close to absorbing what he *has* recorded and released? Melodies. This is a man who almost built an entire album around one melodic riff ("Heroes and Villains"), who can just as easily include enough

151

separate melodic ideas in one song to last most rock groups their entire career. Mystery. Magic. Listen. I think perhaps the post-ambitious period represented on Disc 3 is the most rewarding because it is such a direct link-up with the child consciousness at the heart of this (and every?) great musician. Music for music's sake. Just fooling around. Just trying to talk to you.

Disc 4 is the "wilderness" era: the Beach Boys don't know who they are, Brian doesn't know how to make records or if he wants to make records or who he is, and the years roll by. The first three discs take us from 1961 to 1971; the fourth goes from 1972 to 1988 (and it might as well be 1993). Brian's 1988 solo album is not represented here, since this is a "Beach Boys" collection, so we can leave the successes and failures of that effort to be discussed another time (basically it's a very listenable disc full of wonderful Brian moments but almost every track is crammed with co-producers trying to help Brian finish what he's apparently lost interest in). The live Beach Boys, who were so wonderful in concert in 1974 when *Endless Summer* put them back on top for a little while, are unfortunately not represented here, and what we get instead is selections from the relatively few albums the Beach Boys made over this 20-year period, only one of which was truly memorable . . . Brian's charming return to form, *The Beach Boys Love You*, which went unnoticed at the time and is not currently available on CD as far as I know.

And yet, perhaps just because the good bits have been so carefully selected from a long dry period, and maybe also because these later Beach Boys explorations and evolutions deserve more attention than we tend to give them, Disc 4 is surprisingly rewarding – not close to the quality level of the first three, but still a pleasure to listen to again and again.

This confuses me. If I love Discs 1–3 because they're full of great recordings (Brian's medium was not the song or composition or arrangement or performance but the *recording*, that

152

was what he saw himself creating), why do I waste my time with Disc 4, which contains no major works and very little to compete with the long list of Disc 3 wonders? I'm not sure. There are plenty of good melodies here, including some oddball unreleased tracks that are still growing on me, notably "Still I Dream of It" and "Our Team." The best songs from *Carl and the Passions* and *Holland* are here and well worth discovering or rediscovering: "Trader," "Funky Pretty," "Marcella," "You Need a Mess of Help to Stand Alone," and "Sail on Sailor." (The two albums have been switched chronologically on the disc, for no apparent reason.) I also like the spacey "All This Is That," and it's quite nice to have Brian's "Fairy Tale Music" without the narration. Nice, but not a major event: it's a composition by a man who clearly doesn't have the energy to write a soundtrack or compose a concerto or record a "Good Vibrations." And there are a couple of Brian tracks here I actually would rather not listen to; I've never liked his hit arrangement of "Rock and Roll Music," and "That Same Song," which he sings, is equally irritating. But still there are moments all over this disc that do pull me in, particularly the four songs from *Love You.* "I'll Bet He's Nice," for instance, seems to me as fine an example of Brian's crude, inventive musical exuberance as "Friends" or "Let Him Run Wild." And "Airplane" to me is irresistible. But I wouldn't start a new Beach Boys listener out on this stuff. A disc for fans.

And Disc 5 is a fan's disc of quite a different sort, weird and wonderful and full of revelations. Would you like to have been standing in the studio while Brian supervised the recording of "I Know There's an Answer," "God Only Knows," or "Good Vibrations"? Now you can be, and the experience is anything but a disappointment. I know of engineers and musicians who have been studying these session tapes like holy writ ever since the box set came out. On "Hang on to Your Ego" ("I Know There's an Answer") and "God Only Knows," we hear Brian conducting a roomful of first-rate orchestral musicians,

153

coaxing performances out of them ("Do you think we could hear a little bit more harmonica in that instrumental break, I don't know?" he asks, and the solo that results is one of the great dadaistic moments in modern music), complaining about a rhythmic phrase that isn't going down to his liking and then getting a suggestion from a musician and incorporating it immediately with exhilarating results. We hear him trying on musical phrases and combinations of instruments and alternate angles of incision on fifteen minutes of "Good Vibrations" takes, and although it's a bit much for casual listening, when you can give it your attention it's absolutely riveting, more than an education, more like a personal tour of one of the wonders of the world conducted by the architect/contractor who built it. Best of all, for me as a listener, is the quality of the music itself, "Hang on to Your Ego" just gorgeous before as well as after its brilliant and imaginative transformation into the piece of music it was meant to become. There are parts of "Good Vibrations" not included on the finished track that are pure treasures, the "hum de ah" chorus being my personal favorite, at least this week. And although there's no talk, it's wonderful, in terms of listening pleasure and mental stimulation both, to have pieces of tracks from "Heroes and Villains" and "Cabinessence" and "Surf's Up." Certainly Brian's most beautiful and inventive instrumental excursions were created to serve as framework and backdrop to foreground vocals.

Along those lines, I am very pleased with the seemingly gimmicky set of five songs on Disc 5 that can be heard as pure vocals or pure backing tracks as you switch your stereo "balance" knob back and forth. *Stack O' Tracks* was a fine album and a great idea, but now at last we have *Stack O' Vocals* as well, and the only thing is, I want more. Listen to that backing track for "When I Grow Up" – outrageous! And then those vocals, and then the amazing ways they both come out so different when they're put together. I find the vocals for "Wouldn't It Be Nice" particularly intriguing (and at times

154

hilarious). "Wendy" and "All Summer Long" are also tasteful choices for this "toy microscope" section of the box (kids! you be the producer! what would you have done?). And I tip my hat to the pointed sequence of tracks from "I Get Around" and "Dance Dance Dance," the former sounding remarkably similar to the latter, something you'd never begin to guess from listening to the finished records. What it shows is that the revolutionary structure and sound of "I Get Around" is entirely in the vocals and in their relationship with the music; it can't be heard on the track at all. "Dance Dance Dance" (the first tracks for which were laid down a month before Brian cut "I Get Around," and then put aside until six months later) is much less of a song in my opinion, but the track as heard here is far more lively and musical. (It would have been nice to have had more information on this Disc 5 stuff, particularly as much identification as possible of the different segments of "GV" and the *Pet Sounds* tracks in terms of which takes we're hearing, and from what dates. Obviously we were going to listen like detectives; throw us a few clues . . .)

The demo of "In My Room" is a delightful touch. The live tracks that close the box set are well-intended, but too brief for the listener to really get into (three tracks from a 1964 show, one each from concerts in 1966 and 1967). "Interesting" stuff (i.e. the first live "Good Vibrations" and the last live Brian appearance with the original group), but the compilers of the set don't seem to be fans of (this kind of) live music, and I think don't really realize that an earnest search of the Beach Boys archives and fan's tapes would turn up some superb concert-length performances (which ideally would be presented to us listeners with most of the between-song patter cut out). If we had to be limited to a few samples of live Beach Boys, I would have preferred more emphasis on the beauty of the voices (the 1967 "Surfer Girl" *is* quite special) and the enthusiasm and inventiveness of the band, on a good night before a responsive and intelligent crowd. Oh well. It's an absolutely fantastic six hours and twenty minutes

155

of music, and the further good news is that it's selling well, which means Capitol may be encouraged to release some of the other unreleased Beach Boys/Brian Wilson material in their vaults, i.e. a collection of BW productions of other artists (released and unreleased), a complete set of *Pet Sounds* session tracks, a lot more *Smile* tracks and other assorted riches. This could be fun. Is fun, is magnificent, is an embarrassment of riches already.

So the moral is, life is imperfect, but an American kid with a CD player and a roof over his or her head doesn't have a hell of a lot to complain about. And even the Beatles only lasted seven years, so why do you keep asking Brian what he's done for us lately? But what an amazing story! And leaving aside the hype and confusion over the *Smile* stuff, how can we listen to the *Pet Sounds* studio sessions or even *Pet Sounds* itself and not believe that this guy, somewhere inside, still has this kind of music flowing through him, and could even still have the ability to walk into a studio, under the right cir-cumstances ("no pressure" – hah!), and get talented play-ers to perform their hearts out for him? The thing about Brian (and I think Lew Shiner's novel does capture some of the poignance of this, although his book is really about us fans, not about musicians) is, as long as he's alive, at any moment he could awaken from his nap and saturate our ears with great music again. I don't think he will, necessarily; for one thing, I think his loss of self-confidence is just about absolute (where do they grow that stuff?), and the precious un-self-consciousness that made possible all his great work in each of the Beach Boys "eras" might also be very difficult to resurrect (although the one track I've heard from Van Dyke Parks's forthcoming album, featuring Brian not as composer or producer but simply as guest lead vocalist, is extremely encouraging) . . .

Uh, where was I? Where am I? Which disc is this? I don't want to stop listening to this album (I know, I don't have to

156

stop, but it's such a great excuse to be working on a "review"). It's Disc 3, actually, in my headphones again right now, and I am ecstatically listening to "Let the Wind Blow" and "Cool, Cool Water" and "Little Bird" and, and . . .

And no, I don't feel satisfied that I've found or expressed the secret of what this music means to me. I can do a good song and dance when I'm talking about a lyric, but what can you say about a melody? Or the sounds of the voices and instruments in "Cool, Cool Water" (1967, one minute and eleven seconds) and the ways they echo off each other? I surrender. I admit my helplessness. (Now I'm listening to "Do It Again"; God, it's wonderful.) I shall go back and consider the matter (what can you say about a melody, except that you worship the air it vibrates in?) for another thirty or forty years. In the meantime, I leave you with the words of another fan, a Mr. John Cale of the United Kingdom, who wrote/sang in his great 1975 song "Mr. Wilson" (not about a British prime minister):

I believe you, Mr. Wilson, I believe you anyway
And I'm always thinking of you when I hear your music
  play
And you know it's true that Wales is not like California in
  any way
And when I listen to your music you're still thousands of
  miles away . . .

17

"There's a Lot of Love in It."

In 1995 I was hired as "pop music editor" of a new audio magazine called Fi, *a pairing that didn't work out for them or me except that it did give me an excuse to try again (after 29 years) to complete a Brian Wilson interview, since they urgently needed a cover story for the second issue. Of course, the other editors were unhappy that what I gave them read more like a conversation than a journalistic "interview." They couldn't understand why Brian didn't talk more like their idea of a serious musician or rock star. So here it is, another visit with Brian Wilson, December 4, '95.*

The best pop or rock album of 1995 – my personal favorite, hands down – is *I Just Wasn't Made for These Times* by Brian Wilson. You can read lots more of my thoughts on this wonderful record later on in this issue, and on the excellent documentary of the same title, now available as a videocassette, and on *Orange Crate Art*, the new Van Dyke Parks album that is somewhat misleadingly credited to Brian Wilson and Van Dyke Parks. It's been a good year for Brian Wilson fans, and perhaps just the first of many more to come, now that he has achieved a personal victory over the incapacitating (and much over-publicized) psychological problems that had disabled him for years.

In 1961, at the age of 19, Brian Wilson formed a group called the Beach Boys which would put out its first single, "Surfin'," by the end of the year, and would go on to be the most commercially successful American musical group of the

1960s. But more than that: insofar as rock and roll has produced great works of art that will endure for decades and centuries to come, the Beach Boys, under the leadership of songwriter/arranger/producer Brian, would go on to be responsible for easily as large a share of those enduring works of art as any other group or artist of the rock era . . . and would also be a huge and ongoing influence on almost all other significant creators of rock and roll art.

When I was a young teenager in 1963, the Beach Boys caught my attention with irresistible hits like "Shut Down" and "Surfin' USA," and my attention sharpened when a jazz critic friend played me "I Get Around" in '64 and described it as the most complex and sophisticated pop music construction he'd ever heard. But Brian Wilson became a personal hero of mine once and for all in late summer 1966 when a Beach Boys single called "God Only Knows" drew me to an album called *Pet Sounds* (#1 on *Mojo* magazine's 1995 list of "The 100 Greatest Albums Ever Made"). So I bought "Good Vibrations" the day it went on sale, and in December 1966 I had the opportunity to meet and interview my new hero, at his home in Beverly Hills, during the recording of the legendary unfinished Beach Boys album *Smile*.

That was a great experience, even though the interview was too stoned to be publishable. And so it was a great thrill to find myself again, 29 years later, arriving at Brian Wilson's Beverly Hills home (a new one, attractive, tasteful, not extravagant) to conduct an interview with the now universally acknowledged maestro of modern western music.

Before we began the session, Brian greeted me ("Good to see you again after all these years!"), not surprising me because I'd been told he remembered me as the young editor of *Crawdaddy!* A moment later, in his kitchen, he looked at me searchingly, and asked, "Where did we meet the last time we saw each other?" I mentioned a recent casual encounter, but that wasn't what he was getting at. "Didn't we see each other at an airport?" he asked. "Yes," I answered, astonished, for I'd

160

almost forgotten it myself, "we met at Kennedy Airport in January 1968; you were there to greet the Maharishi, and we talked for a few minutes and I gave you the forthcoming issue of *Crawdaddy!* with Van Dyke Parks on the cover." What a memory! We went into the living room and Brian, a man very much in charge of his own life these days, announced that the interview part of our reunion was now underway:

BRIAN: Okay, here we go.

PAUL: Yeah. The interviews I'm going to do for the magazine I think will just be about music and the experience of listening to music. So the first question I have is, your soundtrack album [*I Just Wasn't Made for These Times*] is dedicated to your wife and your mom but also to Phil Spector. Why did you dedicate it to Spector?

BRIAN: Oh, that was because . . . first of all, he taught me how to do all that. I never knew, until he came along, what to do. But now I know what to do in the studio. He's really helped me a lot.

PAUL: He taught you . . . you mean, by listening to his records?

BRIAN: Exactly. I would listen to 'em, and I'd say, "Is that a guitar or piano, or is that a horn or a violin or a vocal or – ?" And I'd say, "God, it all sounds like one big sound!" That was kind of an exciting thing to – when I first heard that, you know, when I first heard that wall-of-sound type record, really took me quite far away. Took me out of reality.

PAUL: Of course, you'd hear it on the radio, but did you have like a little record-player that played 45s?

BRIAN: Yeah. I wore it out, I wore all those records out. Yeah, I did, actually. There were a number of records that he made that I liked, but I believe "You've Lost That Lovin' Feelin' " is probably my favorite of his records. And then a close second would be "Walkin' in the Rain." You know.

PAUL. Right. "Be My Baby" . . .

BRIAN: Oh, of course, that's always very current.

PAUL: Yeah. I still love "River Deep, Mountain High." Of course that's a little later, but . . .

BRIAN: Right. He wanted to produce the group, the Beach Boy group, when I say "the group" I mean the Beach Boys. About eleven years ago. And my manager turned it down because he wanted too much production money, he didn't want us to get any artists' royalties, or something like that. He wanted all the artists' royalties and all the producer's royalties. And we'd just get a little sum up front for it. And we said, "No thanks, Phil." It was an experience, of course. Think – wow, if he'd produced us that would be an automatic number one record. But it was not a fair deal. Just wasn't fair at all.

PAUL: That's how he's done things in the later part of his career, definitely.

BRIAN: He wants it all. But that's him, that's cool. He will go down in history as something that . . . I was one of the first persons that really noticed his records. I think. I might have been. 'Cause when people heard "Help Me, Rhonda" they said, "Phil-Spector-type," you know, all those instruments going, you know, so . . . Immediately people in the business related us to Phil Spector. That was good. Because then we could be like Phil Spector's group. And that would be really an honor. And something I think would be the highest honor of my whole life, would be to be considered linked with Phil Spector. As he would have been our producer. But not really. All in fun, of course, and all just in fantasy. For real he never produced "Good Vibrations" or any of our records. He did not produce "California Girls" either. Hah hah hah.

PAUL: When did you start finding out that you could do that, that you could hear two different instruments and put them together, and then when you went in the studio it worked?

BRIAN: With "Be My Baby." When I heard "Be My Baby," I said, "That's brilliant, combination of pianos and guitars." I immediately figured out what it was, and I said, "I gotta do that myself," so I went in the studio and I tried it, and it worked.

162

PAUL: Can you remember something you tried it on?

BRIAN: Yeah! We tried it on, um "California Girls." We went in there and said . . . The musicians were the same guys that Phil Spector used, they were called "the regulars." Those guys were booked solid week after week. They went around the clock for weeks. They made a lot of money but it burned them all out. Those musicians played a lot of dates. With the "California Girls" session, Hal Blaine was the drummer. The regulars. I don't know, I felt that those musicians were probably honored to work for me, but at the same time I used to joke around, I'd say, "You guys'd rather play on a Phil session than a Brian session!" They'd laugh their heads off, you know. "No, no! You don't understand, Brian Bareena –" And all that stuff. And we had a thing going there for a while, and then it died out. We did have a lot, believe me, a lot of mutual respect going on with the musicians. Those guys were really super, good musicians. Not only were they good musicians, they were great people. They were very special faces, you know. Hal Blaine's an absolutely gorgeous man. And Ray Pohlman, who died, I guess – did Steve Douglas die too?

PAUL: Yes, about a year or two ago.

BRIAN: What happened?

PAUL: I don't know.

On the way up we were listening to *Stack-o-Tracks* in the car.

BRIAN (excited): Oh yes!

PAUL: That was wonderful. I've always loved that album.

BRIAN: Yeah.

PAUL: I like these little notes that you wrote, a kind of letter, in the booklet of a lot of these reissues, when you did the two-fers.

BRIAN: Right.

PAUL: Here, in the *Stack-o-Tracks* booklet, you were talking about the "Do It Again" tracks: "A classic, it had everything a listener could want, sound bliss, rhythm and excitement." I really agree, and I thought I'd ask you about "sound bliss," 'cause that's what I hear too. What do you think does that, not

163

necessarily just on "Do It Again," but what makes us respond so wonderfully to certain things?

BRIAN: Um, maybe it's called magic, could be music magic. I don't know. I wouldn't know how to answer that.

PAUL: There was a piece in the first issue of this magazine about the Beatles' CDs, and a lot of questions people have had, like where George Martin said he thought they should have used more of the mono mixes . . . On your reissues, I notice that they did use the mono masters any time they were available.

BRIAN: Yes.

PAUL: And I wondered if that was something that you had any particular opinion about. Are you happy that they used the mono mixes, or does it matter to you?

BRIAN: Well, first of all: mono is where it's at. And, second of all, I think it was the greatest thing in the world. It's all from one sound source, mono, and I think that's basically why Spector and guys like that made it so well in the industry. Because it was the *sound* experience. The idea of mono music was like a whole experience in sound. Of course, I'm deaf in my right ear, so I can't hear stereo. I wish I could, but I can't. My right ear was shot in birth.

PAUL: I knew that. But I think you're right, that sometimes by working in mono you can get almost a truer picture of what the music could be.

BRIAN: Yeah. Oh yeah, I agree with you, I really do.

PAUL: Of course, we all started listening to rock and roll on a car radio or something like that, or a little transistor radio. But has it ever been something that concerns you, well, how are people going to listen to this record? Are they going to listen to it on a radio, or on good equipment . . .?

BRIAN: Yeah! Some of the equipment, you know . . . I think if you play a CD you gotta wipe it off sometimes, because it'll seize and skip. You gotta take it and kind of like, very gently wash it, and put it right back into the cartridge, and it'll play all the way through without skipping. I have a Kenny G. album, his Christmas song album – have you heard it?

PAUL: No.

BRIAN: It's great. Really good. And then it starts skipping on this song, so my wife's gonna fix it tonight.

PAUL: Apart from the skipping, do you have any preference between CDs and vinyl?

BRIAN: Oh yeah, CDs for sure. Because, I don't know, I just, it's so delicate, a little circular disc of metal, and you put it on a little player and it plays, I think it's fantastic. It's a whole vibration about it, not just the fact that it's not quite as big around as a vinyl. It's just that vibe of, you know, this delicate little, nice little handy little package, you know what I mean? It's really kind of a cute thing, you know?

PAUL: Did you ever have the experience of like, playing, say, Phil Spector or Motown or something like that on a CD and saying, "Wait a minute! It doesn't sound the way it's supposed to?"

BRIAN: I've, yeah, some of Phil's stuff didn't sound quite up to par on the CDs. I think he made his records mostly for vinyl. I think that's why he hasn't sold very many copies of his records lately.

PAUL: I have the idea, also for like the early Motown records, that they would make this great sound where every-thing got squeezed together –

BRIAN: Right, right.

PAUL: in the compression, but then a CD spreads it all out.

BRIAN: Yeah! Well that's – Give me an example of whose music a CD would fuck up.

PAUL: Things that sound great on singles, like all those early Four Tops records or any of those things that Motown put out.

BRIAN: Yeah.

PAUL: Where there'd just be this great sound, like "Dancing in the Street."

BRIAN: Right, right!

PAUL: By Martha and the Vandellas, and it goes "Crash, crash, crash!" But then sometimes on a CD everything is spread out so much that you don't have the same feeling, in terms of a single anyway.

BRIAN: Right! Yeah. You don't feel it as well. I guess. Who knows? I like CDs, though, for the most part, but when it comes to Phil Spector's . . . I have all his records on my juke box. Not the CD juke box, the Rockola. The Seeburg, 1958 Seeburg.

PAUL: You have a juke box that still plays 45s.

BRIAN: Yeah, 1958 Seeburg. I have "Be My Baby," "You've Lost that Lovin' Feelin'," "Walkin' in the Rain," you know, those kind of records. "Da Doo Ron Ron." And they sound *great* on a juke box, really good, really good. The sound coming out of there . . . the sound just comes out of it, like it jumps out of the box, it just jumps out of the speakers.

PAUL: What else have you got on that juke box?

BRIAN: I've got "What the World Needs Now Is Love, Sweet Love" by Jackie de Shannon. I have B. J. Thomas, "Raindrops Keep Falling on My Head." "At the Hop," by Danny and the Juniors, and "Why Do Fools Fall in Love" by Frankie Lymon and the Teenagers. I have "Baby It's You," that Burt Bacharach wrote, by I don't know, a female group, a girl group. It goes, "Many many nights roll by, I sit alone at home and cry, over you, what can I do? I can't help myself [Brian is speak-singing!] 'cause baby it's you." What a record. What a great record! [by the Shirelles.]

PAUL: Did you put any of your own records on your juke box?

BRIAN: No. Not on the Seeburg, the 45s. On the CD juke box, I have the *Party* album and *Stack-o-Tracks*, all on one CD. That's all I got, just a little bit of that, you know. The rest of it's all, um, Beatles and you name it, Beatles, the Chipmunks, believe it or not, which are a cute group. And that's about it, there's a lot of different kinds of CDs.

PAUL: I like the Chipmunks. Did you know that Simon in the Chipmunks is named after Lenny Waronker's dad?

BRIAN: No.

PAUL: Lenny's dad was the president of Liberty Records, that put out the Chipmunks, I believe his name was Si Waronker, so David Seville named one of the Chipmunks Simon.

BRIAN: No kidding? I'll be goddamned!

PAUL: What an honor.

Cindy, my girlfriend, just went out and got a Four Freshmen record, because I think she'd heard you talk about them in some interview somewhere. And it sounds great.

BRIAN: Which one?

PAUL: I don't remember.

BRIAN: I've got this one called *Voices in Love*, which I think is probably the greatest single vocal album I've ever heard in my whole life. Twenty times better than the Beach Boys, I know that. Unbelievable! It's way, way, way unbelievable.

PAUL: When did you start hearing it, did your Dad . . .?

BRIAN: My Mom. My Mom turned me on to them. She turned the radio on, she goes, "Hear that song? This is called 'Day by Day' by the Four Freshmen." And I listened, I went, "Oh I love it Mommy! I love it. I love it!" So she bought it for me, she took me to the store, she goes, "You can take an album, go in this little booth called a demonstration booth, and you can play it, and if you like it you buy it, you know?" And so I went in there, I listened to the whole album in the booth. I walked out and went, "Oh please, can I please have it, Mommy? Please buy it." I was so out of my mind, after hearing that Four Freshmen thing. So then I'd come home from school, I'd go, "Aw, fuck doing homework, I'm gonna go listen to the Four Freshmen!"

PAUL: Yeah. People who make music are also people who listen to music and love it, it just naturally goes together.

BRIAN: Yeah. Yeah. Yeah. Yeah.

PAUL: In the notes that you wrote for the *Pet Sounds* reissue, you talked about making the tracks and said something about how you wanted to create some sound experiences –

BRIAN: Right.

PAUL: for people. And of course you were very successful in that. I was wondering if you can remember that feeling at all, of wanting to create sound experiences.

BRIAN: Well, I did that because, obviously because I was *really* taking Phil Spector's type of records and making them Beach Boy records. Basically what we were was his messengers. A lot of people knew that, but there are people who probably don't know that, you know. But that's okay, it's just a little bit of trivia, it's interesting. I've always thought of myself as a Phil Spector disciple. For sure. I always have. That's my natural place to be, in the music business, just to kind of be in his shadow, so to speak. [laughs]

PAUL: And I'm sure you realize that there are a lot of other musicians who feel the same way about you.

BRIAN: I know, there have been a number of guys who've come and said, "Brian, *Pet Sounds* is the most beautiful album I ever heard." And I say, "Yeah, there's a lot of love in it, you know," and they go, "Yeah yeah." But there was, there was an extremely lot of lovingness in those records. There's something about them that just felt so loving.

PAUL: It's really wonderful the way that sound can communicate such deep feeling . . .

BRIAN: Oh, of course.

PAUL: To talk about feelings is very difficult, and –

BRIAN: It is! Yeah, you're right. It's like anybody else, somebody goes, "Ah, what do you see, Stevie Wonder?" "Um, I don't know, you know . . ." It's like, say, you try to tell a blind person what something looks like or what color . . . It's like, you can't, you gotta listen to the music to understand what the music is.

PAUL: That's been my challenge all my life, since I started writing about music when I started *Crawdaddy!* when I was 17, and it was always, well, how can I do it? How can I talk about these Bob Dylan records or these Beach Boy records and tell people why I like them so much, you know?

BRIAN: Right.

168

PAUL: There must be some way to talk about it . . . And it's fun, it's still a challenge.

BRIAN: Oh, for me too. I have that same thing.

PAUL: David Leaf said he thought you'd been listening to some crooners recently?

BRIAN: Oh yeah yeah, just uh Willie Nelson, and Rosemary Clooney, those two. My two favorite artists of all time, Rosemary Clooney and Willie Nelson. We play them all the time.

PAUL: What do you like about them?

BRIAN: Well, to tell you the truth, Willie Nelson is, just has a little bit of a nasal sound, just enough to intrigue me. It's unbelievable. There's just something going on there that I like. And I think my brother and my cousin feel the same way. About Willie Nelson. We did a thing with him, we did a record with him. "The Warmth of the Sun." He sang the lead and we did the backgrounds. We did it about a month ago. It's gonna be on an album called, I don't know what it's gonna be called, but there're gonna be twelve different, separate country artists with the Beach Boys backing 'em all up. I'm going to Chicago Thursday to start working on that. I want you to hear this . . .

PAUL: I'd love to. You're producing or co-producing that album?

BRIAN: Well, yeah. Kinda.

PAUL: Rosemary Clooney, what do you hear in Rosemary?

BRIAN: Rosemary Clooney, I hear a woman, who has a whole-hearted love for a man. A very loving woman, who wants to be good to a man. No bad. I don't think there would be any hard feelings with Rosemary Clooney. About men, you know. If there are, she sure doesn't show it, you know. Because she sounds like she's giving her heart and soul to it. I really like her a lot. I've never met her, but I used to love her when I was a little kid. Gosh. [sings:] "When you wish upon a star . . ." I thought, wow, nice.

PAUL: So what you're listening to, is it a collection of hits, or – ?

BRIAN: Just an album called, *Her Best Requested Songs*, or something like that.

PAUL: In one of the twofers you said, "music is God's voice."

BRIAN: In a sense, that's true, but in another sense it's not. I didn't even make that up, a friend of mine said that, he was being interviewed and he said that, and then I picked it up and I said that.

PAUL: Well, I believe it, and what I was thinking is, even just hearing you talk about Rosemary Clooney, that in a way listening to music can be a kind of a spiritual teaching for us, sometimes.

BRIAN: It can help, yeah. The records we play all give us strength and power. There's like a power thing to it. It's amazing. I think.

PAUL: Yes. So I hope that you feel some satisfaction in knowing that there are some people who get that from records that you've made.

BRIAN: Really? I never knew, I never actually knew if people thought that, in my life. I never asked anybody. [laughs]

PAUL: I know a lot of people, including myself, who absolutely treasure so many of the records that you've made, and not just in the sense of thinking that they're good, but that it really helps them in their lives, to be able to hear this music. The most obvious examples are other musicians, when you see so many people even like John Cale of the Velvet Underground or members of the Who, that you'd think it's a different kind of music, but they're so inspired by listening to the Beach Boys. And then they in turn go on and make music for somebody else, partly out of that inspiration.

BRIAN: Yeah. The same way we did with Phil Spector.

Here's something for you that you might like. [getting ready to play me a tape, just as he played me acetates of *Smile* when I last visited him at his home, Beverly Hills, December 1966.] I think that Willie Nelson really did a good job.

PAUL: Was he fun to work with, Willie?

BRIAN: Yeah. Let's get the interview over so I can play you

170

something, you won't believe it. You will not believe what we're going to play you now. [His wife Melinda is finding the tape.] If she finds this tape, you will not believe it. It is the greatest thing I have ever heard in my whole life. Willie Nelson did the lead to "The Warmth of the Sun" and we backed him up, *very* spiritual, *very* beautiful, spiritual.

PAUL: Did he know the song already?

BRIAN: Oh, he knew the song, yeah.

PAUL: I like the version on the soundtrack album, by the way, too. I'm so happy with how wonderful that album is, I listen to the whole album and it just makes me feel good, all the way through.

BRIAN: I know. There's a wonderful thing to it, yeah, I can understand that.

PAUL: Most of that are just things that were recorded kind of quickly?

BRIAN: Yes.

PAUL: And as I say, I really like it, but for you, because the results are so successful, I just imagine that you must have enjoyed the experience, even though it's so different from going in and planning everything yourself.

BRIAN: Right. Yes. That can be possible, yeah.

PAUL: Did it feel different – of course I could ask that about Van Dyke's album, but that's different – to feel yourself, "I'm here to be a singer today." [chuckles]

BRIAN: Yeah. [laughs]

PAUL: Now you've got two albums on which you're primarily a vocalist . . .

BRIAN: The documentary album, and *Orange Crate Art.* I know. There's a certain amount of paranoia that goes along with being a singer . . . [laughs] You know. But that's true.

PAUL: [a few minutes later] We just listened to Willie singing "The Warmth of the Sun" with the Beach Boys, it's really wonderful. Always when I've listened to the Beach Boys I've been interested in the emotional quality of the voices.

BRIAN: Yeah.

171

PAUL: And I've always felt that there was *information* in it in some way. And just now, I really like the way that Willie's voice sounded specifically with the Beach Boys, with those backing vocals, as though there was some magical relationship there.

BRIAN: Yes. There is. Background singing, I believe – that really helps out your lead singers. A good background vocal group is the key to a record, a smash record. I think. I dunno . . . Who knows?

PAUL: Both in terms of inspiring a good performance from the lead vocal?

BRIAN: Yeah.

PAUL: And also somehow filling in something

BRIAN: Right.

PAUL: that we need. Isn't it wonderful? I always suppose that in a way this all comes from gospel, in the American tradition.

BRIAN: Right. It does. The gospel music of America is very very good.

PAUL: When you and Mike wrote this song, "The Warmth of the Sun," and of course he's often talked about the experience of the president [Kennedy] being shot and then sitting down and writing the words. Do you remember, did he just give you a poem, a set of lyrics, and then you . . .? How did the music come? What do you remember about that process?

BRIAN: Well, I tried to write something that had something positive about it, even though it was a sad time, to try to make a positive music that makes people feel stronger about his death, the better to handle it.

PAUL: Did you start working after Mike already wrote the words?

BRIAN: No. We did it spontaneously at my office. That night, the night of November 22nd, 1963. I was at the piano, he was sitting in a chair next to the piano, on my left. And he would say, "dah doo dah doo . . ." He goes, "Wait a minute, I'm getting it. What good is the dawn that grows into day?"

172

And then we took on a whole like extrapolation, you know.

PAUL: "What good is the dawn" sounds like you talking. So did you –

BRIAN: No, Mike thought of that. All of the lyrics were Mike's, he did them all.

PAUL: So you would start finding a melody and he would be finding words at the same time?

BRIAN: Almost, but not quite. Not that fast, no, but almost as fast as that.

PAUL: Because the melody somehow has to fit the words, rhythmically, so did he then find words that would fit into the spaces in the beat of what you were playing?

BRIAN: Yeah. I would sing him a melody, and the course of the melody. Then he would take, instantly think [snaps fingers], "I'll put it like this," he'd go, "Bip!", and he'd write the line. Real fast. It only took us at the most a half hour to write the song.

PAUL: Did it start with the the title, did he come up with the words "the warmth of the sun"?

BRIAN: Yeah.

PAUL: So when he heard your piece of music he came up with those words?

BRIAN: Yeah. After the first verse, he did.

PAUL: First, "What good is the dawn . . .?"

BRIAN: "That grows into day . . . but I have the warmth of the sun within me at night." And then he said, "we'll call it 'The Warmth of the Sun.' " And he kept going.

PAUL: Did that kind of influence what you did musically with the chorus, because then that became the chorus, too.

BRIAN: Right. That's how he did it. He did one part and then he'd get a title and fill in the rest. That's how he does it. He's really a great fast flow writer, very very fast writer.

PAUL: He'd give you some more words and then you'd try them?

BRIAN: No. Melody always came first. I always had to play him a melody to get words. He didn't think of any lines without a

173

melody. That's how he does it. He does not experiment around, he waits for the melody and then he does it.

PAUL: The words to that song are great, as the whole song is. Did you feel that in some way he was expressing what you were feeling, that he was finding words that spoke for you?

BRIAN: Yes. He might have been doing that, without my knowing it. I don't know.

PAUL: Well of course he had his feelings, too. Everybody remembers where they were when they found out the president was shot, so everybody had strong feelings . . . But it's very interesting to think about how songs come into existence. I mean, everybody wonders about Lennon and McCartney, and how did it happen. Of course, sometimes one way and sometimes another way. But you say in your experience usually it would be a melody first and then, when you and Mike worked together, then he would find words that just seemed to fit it?

BRIAN: [nods.]

PAUL: And then you had the song. Do you remember how quickly you guys went into the studio with it?

BRIAN: Not quite. I think maybe about two or three days. We went in there right away, we couldn't get any studio time, but we finally got in the studio and then we did it! I remember we had a hassle about getting studio time, but when we did we got it, it was cool.

PAUL: And then you had to just teach the musicians what you wanted immediately, and get a track down?

BRIAN: Yeah.

PAUL: The reason I'm asking you these questions is just that it's fascinating to think back on the history through which something magical like a song comes into existence.

BRIAN: Yeah right. It is quite amazing.

PAUL: You had the song, you and Mike wrote the song, and then does it just sort of come naturally to you, "Oh I know what I want the boys to sing on this"? "I know who I want to sing this."

BRIAN: Yeah. Yeah. Yes, really.
PAUL: So there's this feeling of being guided sometimes?
BRIAN: Right, exactly!
I gotta have a wrap-up here . . .
PAUL: Thank you very much.

18

How Deep Is the Ocean?
New Soundings from the Master
(*I Just Wasn't Made for These Times,*
Orange Crate Art)

This was written in January 1996, for the same issue of Fi *that contained the interview (nice cover photo of Brian with his chin resting on the heel of his hand and his eyes fixed intently on the viewer, like a goofy holy man).*

You could start here. Even if you're one of those rare souls who has not already encountered and become entranced by the music of Brian Wilson (it is possible, in the sense that we must know there are persons who truly love music who've lived to a fair age without really encountering Beethoven or Miles Davis), you could start with his new solo album, *I Just Wasn't Made for These Times*, and fall in love forevermore with that feeling you get only from listening to this particular music. Brian Wilson's music. And if you already know that feeling, you'll be thrilled to know that it's back, in full force. *I Just Wasn't Made for These Times* is 29 minutes of music as pretty and soothing and gratifying and inspiring as any album Brian Wilson's been involved in other than his masterpiece *Pet Sounds* – yes, equal to *Today* or *Surf's Up* or *Wild Honey* or *Shut Down Vol. 2* or (except for length) *Endless Summer* or the phenomenal Disc Three of *Good Vibrations*, the 1993 Beach Boys box set.

It came as a surprise to me. A guy I know who loves Brian's

177

music as much as anyone poor-mouthed it to me, giving reasons that sounded reasonable. So I wasn't expecting much. And after all, I knew it was just a soundtrack album for a documentary. But in fact it's so much more than that description implies. And I think my friend was suffering from a condition I've encountered occasionally among earnest fans: being blinded by one's own fanaticism, or in this case deafened, because with this album, far more so than Wilson's ballyhooed and pretty good first solo album in 1988, the proof of the pudding is in the listening. I listened to it, and although I'd already seen the documentary and loved it, I was immediately surprised, when I finally picked up a copy of the soundtrack album, at how thrilled I was by what I was hearing. One great song after another, and invariably one great performance after another, with the most peculiar (a flat-voiced home demo tape from 1976, "Still I Dream of It") the actual climax, most wonderful and awakening of all, and wow, how marvelously the album as a whole hangs together, great sequence, great selection of material (unifying the furthest reaches of Brian Wilson's creative undertakings), a rich tapestry with a unique and near-perfect sonic texture. And a unique, and very human, vocal presence, that speaks to me even more intimately every time I hear it. An absolute triumph for co-producer (and documentary director) Don Was, but only because he has so successfully and unpretentiously midwived this triumphant return of such a mighty spirit. Good news. It just goes to show, don't always listen to your "true fan" friends, they might also have wax in their ears. This brief (same length as an early Beach Boys album; to hear your CD as though it were a '60s LP, think of track 7, "The Warmth of the Sun," as the start of side two) Brian Wilson retrospective album is a superb listening experience.

I fell in love with records when I was a teenager because I did encounter, more than once or twice, albums that made me feel this good. And that seemed to speak to me so sweetly and so encouragingly and so arousingly, and so directly. "This

178

person (or this group) knows what I'm going through. And so do I, now that he's expressed it and helped me feel it." What a release. And life ever since then has been a continuing search for more of the same. They don't come along all the time, but when one does come along, that's big news in my little world. (And since I get to write about the records I like, I get to pretend that it's world news: "Life Discovered – or Rediscovered – on Planet Paul.")

"I Just Wasn't Made for These Times" is like the records I first fell in love with because it sounds good, very good, almost every time I listen to it, no matter what mood I'm in. And because sometimes (more than twice) I've had ecstatic experiences listening to this album. That's what got me into this hobby (a life dedicated to listening): early ecstatic experiences that I wanted to repeat. Why we love recordings is that sometimes they actually do allow us to repeat ecstatic experiences. Maybe not every time; but now and then is quite good enough, thank you. And this thrill is legal!

I'm glad the subject has come around to the Beach Boys so quickly in my *Fi* stewardship. I'd like to think that for many of us the question "Why did you first consider getting high end audio equipment?" can be best answered with a short list of albums or recording artists. I envy Brian Wilson his juke box stocked with 45s; in any case, high on my list would be "Heroes and Villains," "God Only Knows," "Can't Wait Too Long," "Good Vibrations," "Don't Worry Baby" and other Beach Boys tunes. *This* is the music I choose to hear as often and as well as possible. Why? Because it has been the source of so many ecstatic experiences, not a phrase I use lightly.

Let's say you're a Beach Boys fan (hope so) and you'd like to feel you're not alone in your enormous enthusiasm. Or, you don't know their music well, and want to know why people get so excited about it. The documentary film *Brian Wilson, "I Just Wasn't Made for These Times,"* just released by Live Video at an attractive price, is perfect for you in either case. Director Don Was says his film "attempts to explain to the non-musician

179

precisely why the phrase 'Brian Wilson is a genius' has appeared on the lips of three generations of musicians like holy gospel." The attempt is a successful one; and beyond that it's a marvelously paced and edited film, fresh and original and wonderfully articulate (and light-hearted and dignified and moving); really an inspired film, very different from but possibly as noteworthy as *Don't Look Back* in its demonstration of how subtle and effective the documentary film can be as an art form or as a storytelling vehicle.

But before I say more about Was's excellent film (will you want to own it rather than rent it once? I'd say definitely), I want to turn back to the album that was made at the same time as the film (summer 1994), and treat it not as a soundtrack but as what it also genuinely is: a new solo album by a major artist. And a very successful one that offers remarkable and enduring pleasures to anyone who listens to it more than twice, fan or not. Since Brian's true gift is as a music maker ("what he's here for," as his daughter says in the documentary), the album tells his story even more deeply and affectingly and subtly than the film, though the film also is deep and affecting and rich in subtlety.

It's an album of eleven songs, all written by Brian Wilson (with Mike Love and his other collaborators, including his controversial ex-psychologist, and in three cases by himself), all previously recorded, performed anew and fairly spontaneously during the filming of the documentary, with Brian as the primary singer throughout. Re-recordings, like an "unplugged" album. We can hear and mostly see these performances during the film, and so in that sense it's a soundtrack, not in the sense of a score designed to go "behind" other action. It's more as though the film were organized around the recording of these new performances. The effect is one of seeing and hearing him and his family and other well-known musicians (Thurston Moore and John Cale are particularly striking) (even Jim Morrison was a big Brian fan) talking about him at a sort of party where he's giving these casual (and heartfelt) performances now and again.

One song stands apart from the "live 1994" format of the other ten on the album, but it fits extremely well in mood – it's the surprising inclusion, in both film and album, of the original home demo Brian made by himself in 1976 of "Still I Dream of It," a song that was unreleased until a 1977 studio recording was dug up for the 1993 Beach Boys box set. That was a good and pleasantly eccentric version of a rather good song; this version is cruder and also remarkably full of feeling – definitely low fi (even a break in the tape near the end) and very musical and wonderfully emotional. To hear this version is also to hear the blueprint of the huge hit version some enterprising singer is sure to release some memorable day. It's all here. What a great song. Brian may have had a confused lifestyle (and some hard times) in 1976, but to listen to this track is to know that he was in fact still the "genius" he was acclaimed as ten years earlier, a person who knows where every note and sound in a great song must fall in order for the song to find its fullest expression. Except this time he's not demonstrating that as a producer and arranger in a studio but as a daffy at-home performer banging the piano keys and croaking into a microphone. Wow! Oh you snobs of the music world or otherwise who have always laughed at those crude corny Beach Boys, here's another chance for you to miss the point, and thereby miss some of the most powerful and original and influential music coming forth in our era.

Well anyway. Gosh, it just occurred to me: now that Sonny Bono's a Congressman, wouldn't it be great to hear Brian Wilson give a heartfelt (and suitably comic) performance of "Laugh at Me"? He does know what it feels like.

Going back again to those rock albums I first gave my heart to – they often gave the feeling of being thematic, whether planned that way or not, and the best thing was that the themes seemed so perfect (thank you Bob Dylan, thank you Jagger and Richard) for what I was feeling in my life when I encountered them. *I Just Wasn't Made for These Times* also has that charming, affecting quality of speaking about very

181

personal subjects that connect for and are extremely important to the individual listening. This is consciously invoked with the first song, an invocation originally written for the 1968 *Friends* album, "Meant for You." The entire lyrics are worth quoting because they say so much about the singer's intention for his album and perhaps his entire lifetime of musical creation: "As I sit and close my eyes [oh, that perfect melody!], there's peace in my mind, and I'm hoping that you'll find it too, and these feelings in my heart I know are meant for you." OK, Mike wrote the words. But at last we hear Brian sing them, and in my opinion the great mystery of Brian Wilson is thereby addressed and explained far better than has been done by any other commentator. In fact, it occurred to me recently that the confusing thing about this word "genius" is in our culture that means Einstein, and we think it has to do only with great mental abilities. But other cultures, like the Japanese and Chinese, know that the heart also thinks. And what I realized, at last, is that who Brian Wilson really is, always was and still is, is a genius of feelings. He has indeed been gifted with an abundance of inspiration. And a sense of purpose: "these feelings in my heart I know are meant for you." That's why he plays the piano, goes in the studio, conducts, and sings. Listen to his album. The genius of feelings is back.

Thematic music. "I think about the love of this whole world." (Second song, from the underappreciated 1970 masterwork *Sunflower*). Sounds expansive. And *feels* that way too. So much feeling. The most striking statement on the album might be (from "Still I Dream . . ."), "My mother told me Jesus loved the world, and if that's true then why hasn't he helped me to find a girl?" Consider this in connection with "the loneliness in this world, well it's just not fair!" (from "Love and Mercy," first included on his 1988 solo album). Thinking about this whole world, indeed. Brian Wilson's new album is, in my warped view, just as political as Springsteen's *Tom Joad*. Springsteen represents the Downtrodden Dreamers' party. Brian Wilson is the spokesperson, maybe prophet, of the politics of loneliness. He feels. And understands. And registers his protest. "Caroline, No" is another protest, of course. And "'Til I Die" a Faulknerian statement of the indomitable human soul, more joyous and to my taste even more passionate and brilliant here than it was in the fine, quirky *Surf's Up* version (1971). Not mere themes. Very relevant and meaningful ones. "How deep is the ocean?" – Brian's zen koan, whether he knows it or not. "I lost my way . . ." His confession. What sweet singing! This is the story of a Kurt Cobain, rock and roll boy, who's survived.

What about the rock and roll girl, you ask? Listen to "Wonderful."

There's so much more to talk about on this record. So many wonderful threads, like the link between another Brian " 'Til I Die" koan, "How long will the wind blow?" (nod to Bob D.), and the fourth track, a splendid re-statement of 1967's "Let the Wind Blow." Fine work by such beloved L.A. studio musicians (wizards) as Jim Keltner and Benmont Tench, interesting (and controversial because some think they "should" have been conducted by Brian) background vocals, the wonderful family epiphany of "Do It Again" and – I will say more, but first, because this is *Fi*, and Brian, and me, I'd like to focus on some of the moments of sound bliss. Many moments. Big bliss.

One of the more obvious opportunities for ecstasy is, oddly enough, the remake of "Do It Again" (obscure 1968 BBs' single), the very song for which Brian coined the term "sound bliss," in his liner notes to the reissue of *Stack O' Tracks*: " 'Do It Again' was a classic. It had everything a listener could want: sound bliss, rhythm, excitement." That was 27 years ago, and he's talking about the track. I always loved that recording (the cleverest "follow-up" title since the Four Tops' "Same Old Song"), and here we are suddenly in 1995 with a new version that's just as much fun, even though it's not conducted and produced by Brian Wilson (as far as we know, though certainly his presence inspired the singers and musicians), and the backing is not by the Beach Boys (replaced by the closest thing we could possibly have to the Beach Girls, Brian's two daughters Wendy and Carnie) (2/3rds of Wilson Phillips) (their mom was one of the Honeys, who sang back-up on some Beach Boys singles). Just as rhythmic, just as richly and wonderfully textured as a musical, sonic experience (Jim Keltner's drumming is superb and then there's the *sound* of the drum, and of the percussion mix and the bass and occasional keyboards that stretch sonic webbing between voices and percussion). A very, very joyous, perfectly celebratory slice of music, less than three minutes, tonic for the ears. Great to watch in the movie, too, should have been in the running for best video of 1995, fun to actually *see* Brian's energetic, earnest singing and the upward soar of Wendy and Carnie's voices and faces and that great bit of guitar soloing (Waddy Wachtel?) on the chorus. This is where music comes from. And, should we be so lucky or true to ourselves, where it's still going.

Another favorite sound moment for me, from an album that's one pleasing moment after another from head to toe, is Brian banging at his piano on the "Still I Dream of It" demo, what a groove, what spirit! If you listen closely, you'll hear where the master got a lot of his inspiration for writing parts and creating new sounds to put on 45 rpm mono records. From hearing his heart and his fingers play through his own piano. And the way his voice, however charmingly hoarse it may be at this moment, rises from those piano chords, as if propelled by the very energy of their rhythm. Brian Wilson demonstrates the launching pad of melody. And of song.

The next burst of sound bliss for me on the album (among many others) is the track and subtly reconfigured arrangement of "'Til I Die." Great sound. And the singing, of course. There's so much going on on every track of this album. The song selection is one of the most intriguing and successful aspects of the overall picture. "Do It Again" is the only Beach Boys hit, and all the other obvious oldies are dodged. "The Warmth of the Sun" is a popular favorite (B-side) from way back in 1963, and a good stand-in for the more predictable choice (another great Brian ballad) "Don't Worry Baby." The other track from the Beach Boys days, from *Pet Sounds* indeed, is "Caroline, No," not a Beach Boys song at all but Brian's first ever solo single, 1966. We do get one gorgeous *Smile* (and *Smiley Smile*) song from 1967, "Wonderful," although mysteriously Van Dyke Parks's name has been dropped from the songwriting credits on the album and movie ("Say, Mike, what was the name of that lawyer again?"). And three wonderful obscurities for those who really love those Beach Boys albums that never made anyone rich: "Let the Wind Blow" from *Wild Honey*, 1967, "This Whole World" from 1970; " 'Til I Die" from 1971. And two songs, great choices, from the *Brian Wilson* solo album of 1988 ("Love and Mercy," "Melt Away"), songs that demonstrate, especially in this context, the universality of Brian's musical and lyrical interests throughout his career. "I wonder why nothing ever seems to go my way. But every time I see you, I get that same old feeling . . . .." "The world's not waiting just for me." And "Meant for You" and "Still I Dream of It," certainly not obvious choices, but extraordinarily powerful ones. Notice also that, like Bob Dylan's *Hard Rain, I Just Wasn't Made for These Times* is an album that does not include its own famous title song. No need. The sentiment comes through (in all its playful pathos) anyway.

I wrote in 1967 that rearranging the Byrds' singles into a greatest hits album amounted to creating a new message, new major statement, due to the power of experiencing the new sequence. That was long before programmable CD players. But certainly Disc Three of *Good Vibrations* and now this soundtrack have reopened our minds and hearts to Brian Wilson's oeuvre in very powerful and timely ways.

And, not to overlook the obvious, how about the singing? This is an album of Brian Wilson singing Brian Wilson songs previously known only as sung (lead singer) by Mike ("Do It Again," "Meant for You"), Carl ("This Whole World," "Wonderful"), or Mike, Brian and Carl together ("Let the

185

Wind Blow"). And he does sing with so much feeling, so freely, and so well. Co-producer Don Was appropriately and brilliantly describes Brian's singing of the new "Caroline, No" in the liner message Was wrote for the CD booklet: "I hear the weary voice of a man who's been hurled through the emotional wringer and yet, one can plainly discern the youthful sweetness, optimism and goodness that characterizes Brian's soul. It's that very dichotomy that makes him one of the most enigmatic and endearing characters of these times."

This is it. The side of Brian's genius that is present but not as obvious on the greatest hits album *Endless Summer*, and our appreciation of which would not necessarily be furthered by the release of more volumes of unfinished *Smile* sessions – yes, I'd welcome them, I'm just saying there's more to this artist than his legend. There's his brilliant, heartfelt music, very much brought to life on *I Just Wasn't Made . . .* Listen to the transitions (you know you have a great album when one of the chief pleasures is in the transitions). Voices to meditative organ on "Meant for You" right into the plain joyous rock rhythms and choral vocal of "This Whole World." So nice. And perfectly followed by the melodic bridges in that song. Rock, especially Brian rock (or Phil rock) is all transitions. How about "Love and Mercy" to "Do It Again"? "Wonderful" to "Still I Dream of It." You won't get tired of this record. And then, every time you get to the 22nd minute, there's Brian's extraordinary declaration: "I'm convinced of it, the hypnosis of our minds can take us far away." Written by himself. But you'll never convince me that the lines he only hypnotized others into writing ("Oh it's been building up inside of me for oh I don't know how long") ("God only knows what I'd be without you") aren't also signature self-expression. Certainly they are once he produces them. Or, as on this album, once he sings them . . . not those, but how about "don't take her out of my life"? or "love and mercy that's what you need tonight"? – somehow it sounds even more like him now than it did on his previous solo album, the one where he had maybe too many friends helping him be alone.

I Just Wasn't Made for These Times, the movie, tells us very clearly who Brian Wilson has been and who he is now. And so does the album of the same title, and more so as you go on listening to it. Good music: the more you listen, the more clearly and powerfully it speaks. And the themes, as they keep adding together, do reach a unified chorus: my friend Cindy Lee points out that all of Brian's music can be heard as one huge expression of a neverending, never-extinguished search for hope. He does keep finding it ("'Til I Die" is a great closing track, not gloomy as his ex-wife suggests in the movie but actually visionary in its hard-fought optimism). And directly through his melodies and arrangements (conducted or led and inspired) he keeps encouraging and inspiring us; showing us, by revealing his own struggles, how it's done.

Get the soundtrack for your listening and aesthetic pleasure. The best album of 1995, as far as I'm concerned. The film is not quite as epochal, but it is a superbly well-constructed documentary, one of the best I've seen about a modern artist. (It certainly avoids the bullshit that passes for biography in our corrupted consumer culture.) And it is full of pleasures, including Tom Petty and Thurston Moore and Linda Ronstadt and John Cale and Danny Hutton and Van Dyke Parks and an articulate music prof. rhapsodizing about the power of Brian's music, home videos of Brian as a child and young Beach Boy and young father, he and his wife driving through the old neighborhood, Brian doing a minute of spontaneous, hilarious Brian comedy ("I have my fears"). And the music. And an emotional texture that makes the whole thing hang together just like a work of music should. 69 minutes, and worth watching more than once.

Then there's the new album by Brian Wilson and Van Dyke Parks called *Orange Crate Art*. It's Van Dyke's best album in many years, a slightly self-conscious but very friendly and tuneful slice of nostalgic Americana (Californiana particularly).

The tunes grow on you. Parks wrote them all except one song by Michael Hazelwood (who contributed lyrics to two of the others) and the closing track, Gershwin's "Lullaby." Wilson is credited as co-creator because he does most of the singing on every track (except the last, which is instrumental). Parks arranged and produced every track. It still might make sense to call this a half Brian Wilson album if Brian's presence were at all discernible in his vocals. There are moments – a nice squawk on "Wings of a Dove," some playfulness on "San Francisco," but they are brief and elusive. Brian's singing is technically fine, which seems to please Parks who seems to imagine himself as Henry Higgins in this case, but Parks has not managed to bring out Brian's signature ability to communicate feeling through his voice, although it is unstoppably present throughout the Was album. Still, Wilson has done a good job of helping Van Dyke make a pleasing Van Dyke Parks album. The incontrovertible indictment of Parks's album as a contribution to the Wilson opus comes in the documentary (just the film, not the album), when we see and hear Brian sing the title song "Orange Crate Art." It's a wonderful song for Brian to sing, and the performance in the film, spontaneous and accompanied only by Parks on piano, is simply superb, and easily 100% better than the version that opens Parks's album. The film version is beautifully and movingly sung. Do we need Van Dyke Parks to teach Brian Wilson how not to sing like that? Gee, I don't think so.

Well all right. *Orange Crate Art* is still an enjoyable album, if you don't go to it to hear Brian Wilson. We do have a soundtrack and a film that are full of the man's heart, and most heartily recommended. And next year maybe a new Beach Boys with Brian Wilson album. Or a "country singers with the Beach Boys" album. Wait and see. Or much better: wait and listen.

19

Smile Is Done

A conversation among David Anderle (Director of a&r, A&M Records) and Paul Williams (book writer) and Cindy Lee Berryhill (recording artist/performer/ Brian Wilson fan and PW's longtime girlfriend), March 20, 1997 in David's office. Recorded for this book. I turned the tape on as Cindy was telling David something her friend Melinda Wilson said recently about her husband.

CINDY: Well, Melinda tells me that Brian's working on an incredible song cycle right now. DAVID: Really? He told me, we ended the phone conversation with him saying, "I've got to get back to the piano now." That's a good sign. PAUL: When I saw him a year ago, he'd done another interview just before the one he did with me. And when it was all over he just wanted to go to the piano to relax. And that's, I think, absolutely standard these days. Just, get on the piano! DAVID: Which is *good.*

PAUL: I want to go back and have you tell the story again about him calling you. I like that. Have you seen him? DAVID: Yeah. We've been in contact. I can't remember when it first started over again, seeing him on a fairly regular basis. 'Cause I would see him haphazardly, every once in a while he'd be on the lot [A&M Records, Charlie Chaplin's former studio/lot near downtown Hollywood] for some reason. I think it started with him calling me one time, out of the blue, after years. We had a lovely conversation; I can't remember what it was, it was very general, and it was a little, not up-tight, but a little tight.

That was followed with being invited to the wedding. That was terrific, going to the wedding. And that's when I met Melinda. Then I think David Leaf was trying to get us together. And I'm just so busy now, it's been very difficult.

So we didn't get together for a while, didn't see him for several months, and then he called again, out of the blue. It was a very funny day, because I had some of my young a&r people in from New York and they were sitting on the couch, and Ellen comes in, she says, "Brian Wilson's on the phone." And they just, like, freaked. So I say, "Is it really Brian?" and Ellen says, "Yeah, it's Brian." So I say, "great!" and I get on the phone, "Hi Brian, how you doing?" and it was just a general, one of those checking-in conversations, great to hear him.

Then, a couple of months after that he was on the lot, he was here with Carnie and Wendy [Brian's daughters], they were doing a record. And my son Jonathan, who as you know is one of the giant Beach Boy fans of all time, comes running in and he says, "God, Brian's on the lot! Would it be okay if I say hi?" And I say, "Sure." So Jonathan went over and introduced himself, said hello to Brian, and Brian said, "Gee, do you think we could go and see your dad?" So Melinda and Brian came in. He looked great. We had a great conversation. It was really fun. And talked about getting together and having dinner, you know, just doing the social thing. I told him, whenever he was available, 'cause he was recording at the time. And then I asked him if it would be okay if I came in the studio and just said hi, and he said, "absolutely."

So I went in the studio, I guess a couple of days later. It blew my mind, because Audree [Brian's mom] was there, and I haven't seen Audree since the old days. He was in with Carnie and Wendy. I brought Jonathan with me, and we just sat there for most of the afternoon, during the session, and it was fabulous. Tony Asher [*Pet Sounds* lyricist] was there. Truly a mindwarp to see all the people. Had a great time watching them work, very impressed with the way Carnie handled Brian in the session. At the end of the session, went over and said hi

190

to Audree, didn't think she'd remember me, and she did, it was great. I was, I am, very fond of Audree. So that was a big upper for me. And then, you know I'm so busy doing what I'm doing now, and things just get busy, and we never get together, Brian and I, but I'd love to get together with him and Melinda and Sherril [David's wife]. We keep seeing each other or bumping into each other or having a phone conversation, now I'd say it's about every couple of months that this happens. But the last phone conversation was, couple of weeks ago Brian called and said, "Hey man, just been sitting around thinking about you and thought I'd give you a call and see how you're doing." I said, "I'm doing great. How are you doing?" He said he was doing really well. He sounded fabulous. I said, "What are you doing right now?" and he said, "Well, I'm, uh, trying to resurrect the music of the Sixties." He says, "You know, that's a very difficult thing for one person to do."

Which I thought was incredible. We talked for a few more minutes, we talked again about getting together for dinner and hanging, and then he ended the conversation by telling me that he, "Well, have to get back to the piano now!" So, whenever Brian says he has to get back to the piano or get back to music, that's time to hang up and let him get there. PAUL: And you know he's building a studio, or having it built. DAVID: No, I didn't know that. PAUL: Yeah. He and Melinda have bought a house in Chicago. DAVID: Really? How'd that happen, Chicago? PAUL: Well, he's got, you know, a new best friend, and it's this guy Joe Thomas, who is the connection that resulted in that Beach Boys-sing-with-country-singers album, and he and Brian have been hanging out together. So I think that Chicago has to do with Joe, but they've bought a house, and it says here in Brian's newsletter that they're putting in "a state of the art recording studio" in the basement. And I know, since we talk to Melinda, that they do go back and forth to Chicago already. DAVID: They're not going to give up the house here? PAUL: No, I don't think so. DAVID: Oh, good.

191

PAUL: And you know also that they have adopted a baby. DAVID: Oh yeah, that was the other thing we talked about that was incredible. I asked Brian how the baby was, and he [D laughs], he said, "Prizewinner. She's a prizewinner. If there were a contest she would win the prize." To hear him talking like that, it's really great to hear him like that. PAUL: Yeah, I really, I admire him. I think it's a big step for a man to, having been through it already, to take that responsibility again and say, "Okay, I'm ready to be responsible for a child." DAVID: Yeah, it's fantastic. It's just another one of those positive moves and steps. I mean, I'm at a point now, I've been at the point for a long time now where I don't even anticipate him slipping back or anything. Every time I've seen him, every time I've talked to him, he's just more solid, you know. And the humor is there. You know, you get to a point where you start looking for little signs of things, and I don't do that. Brian is fine. As far as I can see, Brian is fine. I don't know, medically I certainly don't know anything about him . . . PAUL: Actually, they are even very frank about that in the newsletter in a very sweet way. This is nice. The gal who publishes it for them says, um [turning pages, searching for the paragraph], sorry, I'm lost . . . DAVID: That's okay, that's the way I was, the first interview we did. PAUL: Oh, here it is. Um, Lauri, who does the newsletter, writes, "Melinda says, Brian is the healthiest he's been in 35 years. It's no secret that Brian has suffered from depression in the past. At present, one major medication controls this problem. Both Brian and Melinda want you to know that Brian is just fine! He is positive and upbeat. He is making beautiful music again. The Wilsons have a wonderful relationship and Brian has lots of friends around him. Brian says he is better now at 54 than he was at 44 or even 34."

PAUL: And I mean, it's really true. As you can tell, there's no hype here. It's really like his personal newsletter that his secretary's putting out: "One of the most enduring rumors is that Brian suffered a stroke in the past. This is not so. He has always spoken out of one side of his mouth due to his hearing problem. Also, in prior years, he was on a hodge-podge of unnecessary medication which kept him in a near-sedated state most of the time." So that's it. "Your love and concern is noted and appreciated by Brian and Melinda, but rest assured that all is well with Brian."

DAVID: I've seen that. In all the times I've seen Brian since those days, including some of the times he was still with Landy and still not well, I would have never said that he'd had a stroke. Because Brian *always* talked out of the side of his mouth. You know, even in the great days when we were together, whenever Brian would get that little secret thing or something real special or something sensitive or anything we had to talk about, you know, when he got real serious Brian would always talk out of the corner of his mouth. So when I saw him in the bad days and he was talking that way all the time, it just seemed to me that that was just an emotional thing as opposed to a physical thing. And I watched that dissipate over these last couple of years, and now when I talk to him, that part of it is, it's like the old days.

PAUL: I'm sure that you've probably had an occasion, even recently, to experience how amazing his memory is. DAVID: Ah well, look, let me tell you about Brian's memory. The first time Brian and I came back together again, after those days when we were together, was when he was recording his first [solo] album and he was here on the lot. And he was with Andy Paley and Russ Titelman. I'd gotten a couple of phone calls from Seymour Stein previous to this, telling me that Brian was going to be making this record and asking me if I would spend some time with Andy. And I did, just to talk about the days of the, you know, *Smile* and that whole time. And then when they came on the lot, Russ and Hugh Padgham had come up to my office sort of like to escape for a minute and to relax. Now this is when Brian still had the surf nazis guarding him. We had a lovely time, they invited me into the studio and I went down, with a lot of trepidation and a lot of nervousness, saw Brian, we talked in the studio a bit. It was wonderful, it's

193

always wonderful to see Brian, although I didn't like the way he looked and I knew what was going on . . .

Two days later, all of a sudden Brian appears in my office. I was there all alone, and he came in and we had an amazing conversation. And he was talking about stuff that we did that *I* couldn't even remember. And this was like now at the time that he was supposed to really have been sick, when he was still under Landy's care. The talking out of the corner of his mouth went away, his eyes softened up – it was one of the highest times for me. It was such a great time to see him like that and to have that conversation talking about the old days. Then after a period of time I think he realized, I don't know if he said he was going to go to the bathroom or whatever the case may be, but I think he realized he had to get back to the studio, and he started tightening up again. And I walked back down to the studio with him, and of course there was that little surf nazi sitting there. And then he just reverted back to that other Brian, you know, that ill Brian. But, it was enough for me to know that he was okay. That if he could just get away from whatever was going on, whatever they were doing to him, that he was going to be okay. There was no permanent damage there. That he was probably in worse shape because of the medication he was given at that point than if he didn't have any medication. That's my opinion. PAUL: Melinda says, straight, that he was on the wrong medication then. DAVID: Yeah. I mean, you know, like I said, I had had this conversation with Brian, I just sat there with my mouth open at what he was remembering. He was telling me stories and I was hysterical, I mean it was incredible.

Then, when I read the book, what's the title of his book? PAUL: *Wouldn't It Be Nice*. DAVID: There's a few little things in there about things that went on with him and I that are so dead-on, so sharp, the memory. PAUL: He didn't write the book, but that's another story. DAVID: But those stories had to come from somewhere. PAUL: Some of them just came from our published conversation; the whole book is cobbled together from every source that the ghostwriter could find. DAVID: Which most of the people have done ever since the *Crawdaddy!* talks. PAUL: We won't get into this, but unfortunately now Brian is being sued for the book [by Al Jardine]. DAVID: Right, I just heard that, Jonathan told me that two days ago, I can't believe it. Why don't they just leave this guy alone? This is like unbelievable, what these guys are doing. You know, I think the Beach Boys should just go out and get jobs! [laughter] PAUL: Right. Well, I heard something along those lines that I thought was healthy, which is that Mike has his own band that he takes on the road when the Beach Boys don't feel like it. What was it called, Cindy? CINDY: Mike Love and the Endless Summer Band. PAUL: So at least he can keep doing what he does. DAVID: Well they should, you know, they could drive trucks, they could be selling fruit on corners or whatever, but why don't they just leave Brian alone? I mean, goodness gracious.

PAUL: So I just want to redirect this. I had the thought . . . What we talked about before – And what this really is is like an extension or completion of our original conversation, for the new book. We talked about what happened to *Smile*. And I think we could still talk about that a little bit, from the perspective of now. I think part of the problem is that, because of Dr. Landy and everything else, the subject that everybody [in the press] constantly turns to is, "What happened to Brian?" And I think that's totally wrong [laughs]. Really, you could apply it to anybody. I mean, it's just not as interesting to talk about "What happened to Mick Jagger?", you know. But naturally we can't really expect things to stay the same, for any young artist. And I think . . . My own opinion is, strongly, whether or not it ever gets proven by the product, is, basically, as you were saying, that Brian totally has it in him, and that it's there. I'm not so sure about Mick Jagger [laughter] . . . And Don Was worked with both of them. I loved actually what Don did with Brian, I like the soundtrack album, not just the movie.

But um, the way that our original conversation worked is, we had that great conversation in Paul's bedroom [Paul Rothchild, producer of The Doors, whose Laurel Canyon pad I was crashing in, which is how I met David Anderle, then running Elektra Records' Hollywood office], and that was in November of '67, and then we got together again three months later, at the beginning of March. And even then we got to kind of revise the way it looked to us, based on what we'd heard and what had happened in between. And specifically – again, not that Brian had changed, but I think to both of our credit we were willing to acknowledge that being a listener and an observer, you affect what you hear . . . DAVID: Definitely. PAUL: So this is kind of an opportunity for us to – now it's 29 years to the month since we did the last installment – to take a long view, staying away from this sort of unfortunate obsession that people have with, well, "What's the story about Brian's condition?," or whatever, which I personally think is something of a misunderstanding.

DAVID: You know, what's interesting is that, well certainly from my perspective, my limited perspective . . . it seems to me that the obsession with what has happened to Brian is totally couched in *Smile*. PAUL: Yeah, right. DAVID: I mean, it's a marriage. You know, it's very bizarre, 'cause I think people pin their perception of the downfall of Brian at the *Smile* moment. And the fact that there's never been a conclusion to the *Smile* situation, somehow, to people, still I think leads them to think that Brian is still not recovered. Or not the same person. PAUL: It's a measuring stick. DAVID: Right!! *Smile* is the measuring stick by which these people – and I'm talking, now I'm talking about, what, third-generation kids now? You know, with their fascination for *Smile* and Brian Wilson. Their whole history, or their whole understanding of it, is really based upon the *Smile* legend, or the *Smile* phenomenon, or whatever. PAUL: Right, and the bootlegs they've heard, and so forth. DAVID: And the fact that there hasn't, for some reason there still isn't that *Smile* record. Every, what?, three years we're promised there will be one, there's gonna be a box set, this is gonna be, there's gonna be that, an anniversary thing. And it gets to the point where everyone's anticipating it and it never occurs.

God, I sometimes think if they would just put that damn thing out, then everyone would say, "Okay, Brian's well." Even though he wouldn't . . . it's just a weird thing. PAUL: Actually it's a fascinating example of . . . A guy I knew once said that you create a myth and it turns to stone. And then you have to live with it. DAVID: Yeah. It's like an athlete has a whole career, a great career, and then he does something like an error, or miss a shot, and that's how he's remembered. It's very bizarre how that is. PAUL: Yeah, absolutely, to the point where, then you can have your myth sitting on your shoulders when you come up to bat. And it's bothering you, and the pitcher . . . DAVID: And there's expectations that are other people's expectations and not your own, but you're judged on their expectations and not your own. You're never gonna win, that kind of a thing. Let me ask you a question. Does Brian talk to you about *Smile?*

PAUL: I didn't ask him when I interviewed him. I really didn't want to press him, I think probably I was more cautious than I needed to be. DAVID: 'Cause I don't talk to him about it. When we talk about things, we do talk a lot about the past and, strangely enough, when we do talk about the past it's very personal. It's things that happened with us, and funny little things. And the *Smile* thing never comes up. I imagine at some point Brian and I could sit down and talk about that. Maybe that's what the dinner will be. Because it is unfinished. I mean . . . I did see it actually finished, but never completed. PAUL: It's natural for people, but I disagree, to have the idea that it should be finished. Like you say, it becomes a measuring stick for something. My own opinion, where I come from, is an artist, this includes Bob Dylan, it includes absolutely everybody, is under no obligation to do what his fans or her fans, no matter how much they love the artist's work . . . What they expect doesn't necessarily have anything to do with what the artist has to do.

DAVID: Unfortunately, though, in this case that will always be the measuring stick. No matter what you say or I say or Brian says, or anyone. From now on, I mean from now on from that point, no matter what Brian does now there will be people, the fans, particularly the younger ones, who will use the pieces of the *Smile* music that they've heard as the measuring stick. Which is so unfair, because . . . There's no way Brian can go back and pick up the pieces. I mean, he was, we were so innocent in those days, and Brian for me was like . . . I think I told you [in '67], the magic of Brian was his innocence. I mean, to have that much genius on one hand and that much innocence on the other, and I think that the reason all that genius came out is because he, there was no preconceived notions about anything. I mean he was Mr. Freedom, you know, just whatever came from his heart or his mind, whatever he perceived or any of that . . . That's how *Smile*'s music was made, as we talked about. It was all about great moments, and visions and ideas and thoughts and whatever. Brian would then put it to music, and he would cut that music, whether it was three seconds or three minutes or whatever. There were all these moments.

And that's why I say, to me personally, *Smile*'s finished. *Smile* probably never should have had, it was never meant to have, a shape. As such, a beginning-middle-and-end shape. I think it's just a, a, a large moment of music, of literal musics. And so much of that was sparked by that pure innocence, which he doesn't have . . . I mean, he does have that, I think he probably does have that innocence in terms of, of his *heart*. But I think what he's been through, all these years what he's been through, that innocence is gone. As it should be. Your innocence is gone, that way, you know, you may still have an innocent *spirit*, but you know too much now. PAUL: Right. Yeah, and I believe, and we'll see what he does with it . . . I think it's tremendously encouraging that he's building this

studio, and even, that it's not in Los Angeles, and it's completely free of all that past association, and all the sense of
people looking over his shoulder. Because I think that, well,
we know, and you said this to me 29 years ago, that the way
Brian works is, he wants to be able to go into the studio at any
time. DAVID: Right. PAUL: And to have an actual professional
studio and to have a house that he lives in, where he has, you
know, his wife and his baby there if he wants, *and* the studio.
Then he has the opportunity, not that, as I say, not that he's
required to do it, but he certainly has the opportunity to get in
touch with that un-self-conscious place.

DAVID: See, Brian has to do that. He has to do that, and he
also has to realize, *he* has to realize, that there should be no
burdens on him. There should be no burdens from the past,
there should be no expectations based upon something else.
He should have, if he can, and I know he can, 'cause I know, I
know, I mean I know it, I know he's fine. If he could just again
get to a point where he can just go and make music, period.
And not even have to play it for pros or any – You know what I
mean? Just start making music. But he does need people
around, he does need somebody around, hopefully it's this
guy you mentioned. I mean, I would love to be that person . . .
I can't, it's just not, it's not possible. 'Cause Brian needs somebody there all the time. Even when you're not there all the
time, you have to be there all the time. Because Brian functions really well in the company of friendship. It's a *good* thing
for him. So if he can find this person or these people, who will
encourage him to continue just to make music, and not worry
about what the music means. You know, Is this a single? Is this
an album? Is this for a deal? Don't even get to that. That's
garbage, that's baggage he doesn't need. And that baggage
leads to a *Smile* thing and all that stuff. And I think, I think
that's what he has to do. And he doesn't have to make a record
for Van Dyke Parks, to please him, he doesn't have to do music
to please David Anderle, to please Paul Williams, or . . . He
shouldn't have to do that. Or, he shouldn't even have to please

199

his fans. He's got to get back to that point where he's pleasing the muse. Whatever his muse is. And, uh, I think he's gonna be fine. I think he's gonna be fine.

PAUL: Yeah. The other big measuring stick, and the one that he was obviously conscious of when you read things that he's said over the years, especially in the Landy days, the obvious one, it's the same for everybody in our business, is, "Well, where are the hits?" DAVID: Yeah. PAUL: And for years, during the Landy period, Brian would say, "Well, got to get a hit. I think, yeah, we're working on this 'Proud Mary,' but I think it's gonna be a big hit!" Or whatever. But you could tell, from the way he talked, that he did feel that pressure, and he was confused about it. "How can I be that Brian Wilson that people expect me to be?"

DAVID: He was confused – that's the key. The key is he was confused about it. 'Cause in the conversations we would have about music, he would bring that up every once in a while too. Now, the nature of having the hit in its purest sense, with Brian, is fine. Because that was *his* measuring stick. As to taking something to the point at which he felt it was the best it could be. And that has been confused over the years with getting the hit from the professional record company point of view. Which . . . Well, I'll tell you what. If somebody wants to sit down and debate me, about the music he made, about "Good Vibrations," Brian sitting there thinking about where it was going to be on the charts while he was making it, I'll tell them they're nuts. He was of course concerned as we all were when it came out, that it was a hit record, 'cause we all wanted it to – But mainly to get it to people. It was about getting it to people. And Brian *is* competitive, creatively, I mean he is competitive, and that competitive thing should be encouraged and it should keep going.

PAUL: I think that's perfect, because it's also true of the early Capitol years, regardless of what even Nick Venet may have expected, it's true that this incredible kid, and we still see this happen in the business over the years, was turning out hit after hit, but he was doing it . . . he was doing just what he wanted to do. DAVID: Right. PAUL: There was no way, I mean there's obviously no way that he could have said, "Oh, this is what's gonna go." He wasn't that kind of music maker anyway, of like, "Well, I know how to make a hit record." It was just, "Oh, I have an idea. This is the next thing I feel like doing . . ."

DAVID: Well, I remember so many nights we would be up at Brian's house and he would do something musically, and whether it was Danny Hutton, sittin' around, or Van or whoever was up there at the time . . . we would listen to what it is he had done. And it was a great moment, it was great music, we would listen to it and then we would just carry it to that crazy thing of, uh, "Man, this is *really* good." "It really is?" "Yeah. This is really, really good." "How good is this?" "Well, this is the greatest thing I've ever heard." "Really? How great?" "Well, this could be number one in the country." "How about number one on the planet?" "How about number one in the universe?" You know, and it would get that way. But the joy of it always started with how happy everyone was, and how incredibly good the music was. PAUL: Yeah, and that to me, it's, again, it's a natural, youthful enthusiasm that comes out in that. John Lennon expressed it in the very beginning years by saying, they had this joke, "Well, where're we going, boys?" "To the toppermost of the poppermost!" [laughter] DAVID: Exactly. PAUL: Same feeling. It turned out to be true, but that's sort of a gorgeous historical accident, in a way. DAVID: Yeah. Yeah. Well, lately though Brian has not been able to think that way. When he's being engaged professionally. And everybody is waiting for Brian to have that big, hit record. I'm sure, you know, I'm sure enough people had put that into his head while he was doing his music at that horrible time, that that has sunk in. So now . . .

PAUL: Oh yeah. Because there's no question that also what happens is, you do that and you make a lot of money, and then a lot of people obviously benefit from the money you're making. And you become responsible for them. And whether your next record is a hit or not affects other people's livelihood, including your brothers and . . . DAVID: Yeah, it's like an annuity, twenty years down the line they can sue him again and make lots of money. PAUL: Yeah, I mean it's ridiculous but . . . I've always thought that, not just in the case of Brian but for everybody that we've known that's been successful in this rock and roll business over the thirty years, is that part of the tremendous burden that comes with the success is, look, if you don't feel like going on the road, your road manager isn't going to eat. DAVID: Oh yeah. PAUL: Etcetera, etcetera. I mean, the Grateful Dead had their own way of dealing with that, that they kind of had an extended family, but that's the point. Is that everybody's making some money, there's a lot of different people now who, instead of you just putting down whatever song you feel like putting down, what you choose to do and how it does on the charts – DAVID: Affects other people's lives. PAUL: Right. Not just in terms of they can pressure you, but in terms of that you care, you might have feelings about that. DAVID: Yeah definitely. I see it all the time. And have, and have since the beginning. And actually when I talk to young bands, I talk to them exactly this conversation. You know, "You think things are tough now, wait till you're successful! Then it's going to be tough in ways you can't even imagine. 'Cause all of a sudden people are going to be able to send their kids to school or not, based upon what you're doing."

PAUL: Right. And I also feel that – I love *Wild Honey*, and *Friends*, and *Sunflower* and some very obscure things like *The Beach Boys Love You*. And my point of view, from my knowledge of the business, is that not a single one of those records would necessarily have been released at all if there wasn't the Beach Boys' success and history preceding them. DAVID: Right. PAUL: That as good as those records are, and as much as I like them, if you were just coming out of nowhere, and you brought your tape of *Friends* in, to anybody, your chances of actually getting a deal and getting it out at almost any point in the last thirty years, it just takes sort of blind luck or something. But it's not something almost anybody's gonna say, "Oh yeah, we can put that out. We know what to do with that." DAVID: Well it's certainly still the case, isn't it? We always, sometimes some of us older-timers will sit around and talk about, "Okay, what if the Byrds came in today and they put on 'Turn Turn Turn'?" What if, you know . . . First thing we do is go, "Where does that format?" PAUL: Right. "Yeah, now how are we gonna break this?" DAVID: "Is this a Triple A record?, or does this band tour live and can we afford to put them on the road?" PAUL: Yeah. And so I mean I don't take anything away from the positive aspects of the top 40 nature of rock and roll, I love that and how it's worked. But I just think it's also important to remember that once you're a Miles Davis and you've established yourself as being Miles Davis you could keep putting out these ridiculously adventurous records based on your reputation, I guess . . . DAVID: For a while. PAUL: Yeah, not forever necessarily. DAVID: Not any more. The business now is not the business you and I know; it's a much harsher mistress now. Than it was. It's very demanding. It doesn't have a lot of love for what you did previously. It definitely is, "What have you done lately?"

PAUL: I've been thinking about that a lot, how the career artist almost is something that's not happening now, and it's . . . DAVID: You have to work very hard for a career artist. To create a career for an artist, you have to work really hard. PAUL: And realistically, and this is another subject so we won't go too far off onto it, but realistically, in 1997 anyway, a lot of record companies if they tell you the truth, they aren't really looking for a career artist, they're looking for the next record that maybe you can get six or seven million copies out there. That's what works, that's what makes you look good. DAVID: It's a business about quarters. It is. It's a business about quarter performances. How each quarter performs. And what that means within the whole framework of the conglomerate corporation that you happen to belong to. What does your quarter mean to the rest of the corporation? And we all try to think that that's not the case, but it clearly is the case. And monies are allocated based upon that, and somehow the music, I mean I don't know how the music even lives to be honest with you.

PAUL: Yeah, the paradox is, I mean I could complain, and I do, of course, living with Cindy and seeing what she or what any artist goes through, but the paradox is that, for all the problems – I have to acknowledge that one way or another good music does keep coming out. DAVID: It *has* to. Because art will out. PAUL: Exactly. So it's not like, "Oh, it's killing the music!" Well, no, somehow if you really do the work of listening, you'll find there's still lots of great stuff out there somewhere. DAVID: Absolutely. Art will out. It's hard to hammer it through there, but it does do it. And then there's always a joy when it does get there. There's always this wonderful moment where everybody goes, "Yes yes yes!" and then they forget, and the next, you know, set of problems, fiscal problems, present themselves. 'Cause I'm always running around just being, you know, Mr. Pollyanna, I just run around going, "Well, you know, everything's gonna be fine! Let's just get the record done, let's listen to the music, the music will be, you know, the answer's in the music." And luckily that's happened enough times, people still listen once in a while.

But it is a different world. It is an incredibly different world to live in now.

PAUL: What I'm going to do, the last thing I have to write to finish off this book, and I'm on a short deadline, about ten days . . . I'm going to write an essay about two albums that I love, *The Beach Boys Love You*, and *Spring*. What I want to do, which is what I've always tried to do, is argue for what I hear as a listener. To me, the greatness of Brian Wilson is in these two albums, alongside the other stuff. DAVID: That's interesting. PAUL: And it's sincere, I mean I don't necessarily expect you or anybody to see it the same way, but for me it's like what I

204

love in the early hit singles, or in – Of course there's a perfection to *Pet Sounds* and so forth, but that doesn't mean that I
think that the best of the early stuff falls short of it in some way.
I think there's just a certain level, which I like to think of
in terms of, you're looking at the complete work of Claude
Monet, or someone like that, and whaddaya like? The whole
work hangs together, and then it has these high points . . .
What I'm saying is that for me, when I argue for the genius or
greatness or whatever of Brian Wilson, it isn't just based on the
most obviously intricate and complex material, which is kind
of what people are looking for when they're looking for *Smile*
to finally happen or to come back.

DAVID: No. The genius of Brian Wilson is exactly what
you're saying. You've always got that. The other day I was
watching something on television, I was channel surfing, waiting for the eleven o'clock news, and I got the end of some
made-for-TV, or it could have even been a sitcom, I don't even
know any more. But I got the end of something, and it was a
beach, kind of a beach thing at the end, and all of a sudden lo
and behold Beach Boy songs came on playing. And it was so
fresh and it was so right and it was so well-invented. And it was
so *old*! And I just sat there and I said, "This is the genius of
Brian Wilson, that some twenty-some-odd or thirty years later,
this music is now playing and it, it's right. And it's fresh, and
it's exactly the only music I could think of that should be
playing here. And there was one little item, can't remember
which one, one of the little simple surf songs . . . PAUL: Yeah,
it could be anything, "Catch a Wave" . . . DAVID: It could be
anything!

PAUL: Right. And so to me, and this is not at all a matter of
finger-pointing but rather trying – my job, in effect, as a commentator – to change a perspective or restore some sanity. I
personally think that if a record like *The Beach Boys Love You*
was greeted – which I understand it couldn't have been, and I
totally give Mo and Lenny credit for all of the wonderful things
they did for Brian and the Boys and so many other people over

the years, I just feel that they like everybody else were caught in the *Smile* myth at this point. Either one, either the *Smile* myth or else, "We need a hit single!" So you're not going to turn to the artist and say, "Just make more records like this . . ." But I think if somebody could have actually somehow sat down with Brian at that point and really made him feel that it was okay to just do "Honking Down the Highway" . . . And he would have said, "Oh cool! I would love to do more 'Honking Down the Highway' and 'Johnny Carson'!" Or whatever. He could have turned out record after record like that, even in those so-called "bad days." But he didn't feel that freedom. I'm not pointing a finger. I'm just saying that's the way it works. It's difficult.

DAVID: No, you're absolutely right, he was not feeling that freedom because that freedom wasn't there. But why don't we do this? Why don't we just declare, right now, that *Smile* is finished? PAUL: Yes. Excellent! Really. [laughter]

DAVID: *Smile* is done, and Capitol can relax, they don't have to worry about putting out the box set at some point. No, it's done. It was finished when Brian stopped working on it. And that is the way it was supposed to have been. Not released, 'cause it was never, he never, it was just bits and pieces. So, everyone's heard it, at some point or another, but you have to assemble it yourselves. PAUL: Who was it, Schubert, who wrote the "Unfinished Symphony"? DAVID: Uh huh.

It's done. *Smile* is finished. You can have it any way you want it, program it on your CD, put it in random, you know, hit random, let it come up anywhere it wants. PAUL: Excellent. Yeah, Andy Paley's plan at one time, and it could still happen but the point is it doesn't matter if it does or not. It's already done. But his plan was just to put out with Capitol five or six CDs called *The Smile Sessions*. And just like that. And you can program your own. Just take what's there. But don't burden Brian with saying, "Okay Brian, now you have to get back into that state of mind of thirty years ago and figure out what you didn't even know then, which is how you're gonna put it all

206

together!" DAVID: And he's the only one that can do it. See, that's the other thing. The other thing that's so bizarre to me is, is, you know, God love everyone who loves Brian as much as Andy and everyone else does, they're not gonna finish *Smile!* How can they? It's presumptuous even to imagine. I mean, *I* couldn't finish *Smile.*

PAUL: Right. And why should you or I or anybody decide that that's what Brian should want to do?

DAVID: It's done. *Smile* is finished and everyone has it in some form or another, and it's fine. We can relax and move on . . . PAUL: Yeah. In the Bob Dylan world there's a lot of people who are waiting for him to write the next songs to follow the songs that he wrote in 1965 or something like that. I mean, even though they're big fans, that's still . . . And frankly, it just doesn't occur to people to give the artist a break. And say, "Okay Bob, okay whoever you are, do what *you* want to do!"

DAVID: Yeah, right. "And I will judge it of the moment," as opposed to, you know, "Is this as good as *Blonde on Blonde?*" "Duh, this isn't good as 'Visions of Johanna.' " What do you mean it's not as good? It's just not the same. I know, it's weird. It's really . . . it's hard. Maybe all rock and rollers should die early, maybe that is the answer. [laughs]

PAUL: Yeah, that's really – DAVID: Maybe rock and roll isn't meant for longevity. Maybe it is music of the moment . . . PAUL: I felt, for years, and I think it's really true, that not just the public but the critics especially were always angry at Dylan for not dying. DAVID: Yeah, exactly! And for continuing his career. "Not dying, okay, but why are you still making music??" [laughter]

PAUL: Right. Because it's so convenient, it's so easy to handle Jimi Hendrix and so many other people because there's a closure. And then you can totally love it, you know, and say "this is perfect." And then you can fantasize about what Jimi would have done next year and the year after that. DAVID: Right, right, you can invent your own Jimi Hendrix record. PAUL: And it's very convenient for the listener, especially the critic, especially somebody who's going to write about it or anything like that. But even for the listener, it allows you to just say, "Okay, now I know who Jimi Hendrix is." And you're not confronted with having to deal with the weird stuff that you don't understand that he's putting out in 1997.

DAVID: That's really interesting, I was reading this article in *The Times* the other day about Fred Zinnemann after he passed away, and his last years, and when he just stopped making movies any more because everyone expected him to continue to make the kinds of movies he made when he was younger, and you just can't do that, you know. So his later, his last couple of movies, he would make movies and they'd be judged on what he had previously done. And so he just stopped making movies. Period. He just became a president of this and a president of that, you know. And I think that's what happens sometimes. Certainly in rock and roll, that's what happens. You know. I mean, what if the Who decided they were going to make another record, now? Yikes! PAUL: Yeah, well unfortunately they have decided several times in later years to tour, and even the fans will tell you, "Oh dear . . ." DAVID: Yeah, I know. [End of side one of cassette.]

[Side two starts in the midst of Cindy telling David something about her experiences of listening to "*Smile* stuff."] CINDY: I don't know what it was supposed to have been, or anything like that. All I know is that I hear all these fragments and pieces and it sounds fine and done, and it sounds like, you know, orchestral pieces. And it's just *perfect* the way it is. DAVID: And you can play 'em in any way you want, at any time you want, and . . . CINDY: Yeah. And you know, I mean, mostly what I have is like little . . . PAUL: Hold it, hold the thought just a sec . . . [checks tape] Okay, go!

CINDY: I have various bootleg tapes, and um, each one has a slightly different order to it. I just like that, I like the fact that it's so, you know, it's all mixed up and there's no particular order to it, and you just get into the *sound* of the music and not – I mean, it really makes it *great* that in some of the places where maybe it's not done, maybe it was supposed to overlay over another song or something and come together as more of, maybe a pop song . . . But you have all these little pieces and they add up to like these great orchestral moments, you know?

DAVID: It's like a kaleidoscope. CINDY: Yeah. DAVID: Um, Jonathan had a bunch of those same things, those little pieces here and there and he would play them and I would some-times go in and hang out with him and try to tell him little stories (CINDY: Cool . . .) about, if I remembered the night this was cut and whatever. And I, it was *great* to hear them that way, 'cause that's the way we heard them with Brian. CINDY: Yeah!! That's the way, maybe, they're *supposed* to be. DAVID: Brian was continu– you know [to P] we talked about that, he was continually *shuffling* and, when we talked about the *Wild Honey* thing, I think I probably was most disturbed at that time because people had put a beginning and an end on some of these songs [in *Smiley Smile*], and that's not really the way necessarily it was supposed to have been, that song. Remem-ber, I think I was complaining that I thought that the other guys had bastardized some of the brilliance that Brian had had by making *songs* out of these things that weren't quite songs yet.

PAUL: Yeah. Yeah, exactly, because certainly the experience that I had that made me think that *Smile* was one of the most incredible, or going to be, the most incredible things I ever heard in my life, was, you know, Brian played me a scratchy acetate in his bedroom, of something – I don't know what the hell it was, but it was like, whoa! What *is* that?

DAVID: Exactly. It was one of those moments, I'm sure. That was now going to become the bridge of "Bicycle Rider" or . . . which meant he was gonna have to move *that* bridge into something else . . . And that's where it all ended for all of us, that's where it ended, it ended with that kind of moving around of music. And I think that moving around of music is

209

the album, and I think it's the only album ever made that way.
CINDY: Yeah. PAUL: Yeah. DAVID: And it's over. It's done.
Brian is free. Brian can go out now and do something else.
PAUL: Absolutely!

DAVID: Is this guy he's working with a collaborator, or, I
mean is he, what does he do? CINDY: He's a country guy.
PAUL: Well, I don't know much about Joe Thomas, either.
DAVID: I mean, is he a musician or an engineer or a
businessman or – ? PAUL: He's a musician *and* a producer
and . . . DAVID: I think I met him! At that session. PAUL: Yeah,
he was like a co-producer of the Beach Boys country sessions.
DAVID: All right. I think I did meet him. PAUL: And I don't
know much about it either, but he's definitely, I think he's the
Chicago connection. And the neat thing about it is that what's
happening is a studio's being built. It's Brian and Melinda's
house. It's their house, it's their studio. It's a home studio, but
a professional home studio, and at the same time this guy Joe
is there to help, well to supervise the putting in of the studio
and so forth. But, you know, if Joe and Brian have a falling out,
Brian still has the studio. But meanwhile . . . So there's no way
of knowing, of course, in *any* of our lives, what's gonna
happen, but it just feels like . . . to me, it sounds like freedom.
What we were talking about – And also, he has a deal, thanks
to this guy Joe, with River North, which is this sort of, I don't
know if it's Joe's company or what it is, but it's some country
packager that probably makes deals then with other labels, but
nevertheless it's a deal for two Brian Wilson *solo* albums. Which
means he doesn't have to . . .

And Cindy had the experience within the year of actually,
accidentally, walking in to Ocean Way, the old Western
Studios, and finding Brian in the studio with the Beach Boys!
CINDY: A little stunning . . . DAVID: When was this? CINDY: It
was, uh, well it was a year ago in November . . . PAUL: She was
mastering next door. CINDY: Yeah, I was mastering next door,
and I just wanted to check out what's this studio like, I've
heard about Ocean Way and I think it's, used to be Western or

something, and I just had a – DAVID: That's where all the Mamas & Papas records were done. CINDY: Yeah. And wasn't he, was *Smile* stuff done there? DAVID: Yes, "Fire" was done there. CINDY: Ohhh. Yeah.

Well anyway, you know how you can get, like, an intuition? DAVID: Uh huh. CINDY: I just had this intuition, like, I should go in there and ask the receptionist if David Leaf was there. And I did, and they said, "Oh, if he's one of those Beach Boy guys, go on back to studio C." [giggles] So I went back to Studio C, and they were back there. I don't know why, I just, you know . . . I mean it must have been like some kind of like a timewarp, I was thinking, "Oh, this is the place . . ." DAVID: No, it's just, that's what happens. [laughs] That's the thing that happens. CINDY: And they were working, uh, Andy Paley was there, Audree was there, and she'd met me once before and she acted like she remembered me, but – She couldn't have remembered me, I'd just met her briefly in the past, but, and then, uh, Don Was was kind of a co-producer, but he wasn't really doing anything except talking on the telephone the whole time. And I was there for about three or four hours.

PAUL: And that was one of those endless stories that we've heard over the years, like, "Oh, Brian is producing the Beach Boys!" And he *was* producing, with Don Was's help and so forth . . . CINDY: Yeah, he was. PAUL: But you can see, at least it's easy for me to totally understand, probably easier really than it is for Brian himself to understand, how there's . . . You don't have the freedom that you need as an artist when you're like having to carry that whole . . . All the issues involved with, well, it's the Beach Boys, and of course the personalities . . . DAVID: Well, you know that was the big hassle I had with the Beach Boys, was that was exactly my position. I was always trying to get Brian just to be a free spirit. And he would, you know, it would always get to that point where he'd say, "Well they're, you know, it's my *family* and that's the thing," and he would have that responsibility. Whenever I saw that I would just back off. "Absolutely, Brian, it's fine with me. We'll get to our thing later." I mean, I'd understand that, because the last thing I wanted to do was get in the middle of that. But um, he gets to be a different person when it's that thing.

PAUL: So, it's great. I mean, along with declaring that *Smile* is finished [D laughs], I think we, you know, without saying anything we can just declare to the universe, for Brian's sake as it were, that Brian and the Beach Boys are finished [D & C laugh], that making hit records is finished, and so, whatever happens, none of those things has to be carried with it.

DAVID: All right, let's do that. CINDY: That's cool! DAVID: Okay, we've done that. And the message now to Brian is, just go out and make music for yourself. PAUL: Yeah. Yeah, and see what happens.

I wanted to share this with you [P is about to read from the second issue of *Break Away with Brian Wilson*, Lauri Klobas's "fan club" newsletter], because . . . The way I always thought, David, about the conversation we had, that so many people read, was that it was also like, you know the *Reader's Digest* has this series called "The Most Unforgettable Person I Ever Met," and that you were talking, less than a year after your time with Brian, about what an extraordinary impact this *person* had had on you, and . . .. Listen to this. This is from a speech that Don Was gave when he was presenting the Les Paul Award to Brian, at TEC, whatever that is. This was just last November. And somewhere in his talk Don says:

> "I've known Brian Wilson about seven years and consider him a close friend. Yet whenever I think I really know him, I'm reminded that he is the single most enigmatic person I've ever encountered. I once summoned up the courage to ask him what I'm sure is a tedious question; I wanted to know what was going through his mind when he wrote the song "'Til I Die" . . . specifically, what prompts a person to write a song so chordally complex that it is impossible for me to tell you what key it's in. He told me that he was sitting at a piano, creating

212

geometric patterns with his fingers, trying not to move the fingers on the outside of the patterns, but limiting changes to internal movements. When he landed on a shape that both looked cool and sounded good, he wrote it down. So, essentially he created this masterpiece by contorting his fingers into really groovy shapes. Well, I thought that this was one of the most brilliant things I'd ever heard. If I were to sit at a piano for 200 years, I don't believe such a method of songwriting would ever occur to me. But I must tell you that I've absolutely no idea whether this story has any basis in truth or whether he was just making it up on the spot to entertain me."

DAVID: Which is the *other* genius. [laughter] PAUL: And he went on to say, "He is the strongest human being I have ever met, having survived adversities that I'm sure would have killed everyone in this room . . . (umm, that is, unless Keith Richards is here tonight)." [laughter]

DAVID: It's a good speech. PAUL: Yeah. So that reminded me of the Brian that you knew and that we were talking about. DAVID: Yeah, definitely. Absolutely, I mean that's exactly right. That's exactly right. And then, and the kicker is, then after all that not really knowing if he meant it or not. PAUL: Ahaha, right! Yeah, there's some old interview where Carl is saying, "Oh, don't do a put-on, Brian . . ." And there's that whole issue, which people always have with Bob Dylan too, of like, well, is this a put-on or not . . .? DAVID: Right. Right. Is he serious or isn't he serious? I try to do that a lot, too. PAUL: This one, the one that Don just said in his speech, has the ring of truth to me. DAVID: It does. PAUL: It's like it's too ridiculous, it's too absurd for even Brian to think of it as a put-on, because it's – DAVID: Too interesting. PAUL: It's too beautiful. [laughs] DAVID: It's too hard to think that up.

PAUL: That's what I think, yeah. Is that there's certain things like that. I mean, unbelievably, Bob Dylan once explained to me, I mean I just caught him at an off moment, there was no tape recorder, we were just talking ... Uh, explained to me how he'd put together this obscure movie called *Eat the Document*, which then became the model for the movie made later, *Renaldo & Clara*. And, it was very much like what Brian just said, because what Dylan was explaining was that he and his partner, the director Howard Alk, basically numbered types of scenes. They just gave them all numbers, like a #6 would be something with a train in it, and a #5 would be something red, because they were cutting up all this film footage. And so forth and so on, maybe a #7 would be a fan asking a question. And they'd say, "Okay, well, we need a #6 here now." [laughs] And that to me sounds kind of like what Brian was doing with himself at the piano. DAVID: At the piano. And I could see it happening. I could see him looking down at one point and seeing a certain kind of shape, and then get that *brain* of his, the way it works, then wondering what this would, looking at that you go, "Now, I wonder if I could just keep extending that?" And all of a sudden here's a song.

PAUL: Right. And my belief is that then people get this, I mean I thought it was great in the first place for Derek Taylor to come up with the "Brian is a genius" thing, because that helped, as we talked about 30 years ago, start getting people to take him seriously. So I don't criticize that, but I'm just saying the way a myth works is that our minds freeze to stone. And I believe that people who have played an important role in supporting Brian over the years have still, in my opinion, gotten confused by their idea, we all have our ideas, of what it must mean to be a genius. That you must be able ... Therefore they think Brian's not all right because when he's all right, he'll have this ability to go into a studio and do *anything*. Because, you know, for the ordinary person, even if they're not at all an ordinary person but a record executive who's done a lot of brilliant things or whatever, it's still easy for us to get stuck in the idea that for Brian Wilson to create something as great as *Pet Sounds* or for Bob Dylan to write something as brilliant as

"Mr. Tambourine Man," the way that our minds work we think, "Well, he must have known what he was doing." And I say, "crap!" DAVID: Or there must have been a bigger reason for it than just what it is. PAUL: Right, exactly. Whenever people analyse Dylan's work, they analyse it as though the writer had in his mind, "This is gonna mean this, and this is gonna mean that."

And so my whole point is that I think actually most people, including most very smart people, don't quite get, or they forget, that the universe doesn't really work that way. And that genius actually can be about inspiration, not control. DAVID: Or feeling good at a certain moment, and stuff happens. PAUL: Yeah. And then having the courage to say, "I like it," "I like it the way it is." DAVID: That's right, and walking away from it. PAUL: And there were times, David, when I must admit that I felt guilty, I felt, well, Brian is trapped in this myth and I helped create it. I mean, that's silly, but I just – DAVID: Well, you did. And the silly part is to have suffered because of it. PAUL: Right, exactly. I agree. DAVID: But you did, I mean . . . That's why it's important for us to end it right now. [laughter] The record's done, the Beach Boys are finished, Brian having hit records is done . . . PAUL: Right, all past ideas of what it would mean for Brian to be a genius. Good.

DAVID: I remember the first time I saw that in print, "genius" and Brian. Oh gosh . . . PAUL: It was Derek, I think, or maybe not because he – DAVID: No, it was Jules Siegel. PAUL: Oh, okay, because you just didn't see where Derek did it. Because that was part of what converted me, is Derek wrote an article which I read in *Hit Parader*, and he probably wrote it all over the place. DAVID: It was Jules Siegel, and it was in . . . PAUL: In *Cheetah*. DAVID: In *Cheetah*. PAUL: Yeah. See, that's a year later. In summer of '66, when Derek was working with the Beach Boys the first time, he wrote an article which I read actually before *Pet Sounds* came out, or just around the time it was about to come out, asserting, because Derek had balls, he

215

had the balls to say, "This guy's a genius." And then he made his argument.

DAVID: And that probably was spurred by McCartney or somebody saying it . . . PAUL: Yeah, that could have given him the confidence to say, "Okay, I've got my angle." He knew he was a flack, I mean we know Derek, and he was drinking, and he knew he was a flack but then McCartney saying that, he thought, "I've got my angle, I know what I'm gonna go with here!" [laughter] DAVID: "It'll be a nice story, no burden." And then Jules, I know why Jules used it, Jules used all that stuff because it always made him feel like he was more import- ant, because he was the one doing the interview with this genius. I used to have so many fights with him, because he would say, "Well, I'm going to say this about you." And I would say, "No, you can't say this about me, because it's not true." And he says, "No, but nobody needs to know that." And I say, "But everyone's gonna know that if you write it." I'd say, "Why are you doing this, Jules? You're just such a shithead, why are you going to do this kind of . . .?" Well, it really turned out, because if he wrote it then it would make him look important, that he was part of the posse or part of the secret or part of the thing.

PAUL: Of course. We're all like that. Years later, Jules had a piece, that's still twenty years ago probably, in *Playboy,* called "Who Is Thomas Pynchon and What Is He Doing with My Wife?" DAVID: I did read that. Thomas Pynchon was to Jules Siegel what Phil Spector was to Brian Wilson. [laughter] PAUL: So yeah, I'm very sympathetic to Jules, I did the same thing. It's like when you find yourself in the middle of something that you recognize is a myth, how can you resist myth-making about it? DAVID: I guess we all do that. We all extend the story, don't we? We all extend the moment. It's satisfying. But what a burden for Brian . . .

PAUL: A final thing, because when I read over the original piece I discovered that we didn't have the story of your paint- ing of Brian, although you have told it elsewhere, I think Tom

Nolan printed it in his piece. And I was thinking, I want you to . . . well, go ahead, tell that story again, I know you have many times, but just of showing – DAVID: Showing Brian the painting? PAUL: Yeah. You painted it, basically, by yourself, right? I mean, he didn't model for it.

DAVID: No, he did not model. I painted it, I had several pictures of him, photographs, little snaps, and I had an idea of what I wanted to show. And then what would happen is, we would be . . . this is the period of time I was with him every day and every night. And we would be together at night till what, two or three in the morning, whatever the case may be. And then I would come home . . . And at that time I was living in this little garret kind of thing down by USC, with Sherril, and Sherril was working at the time, so we would have enough money to buy popcorn to live on. It was really those kind of days. I would come home and then I would just paint, until I either couldn't see any more, or I couldn't – The thing that I saw in Brian, because when we were talking I'd just be staring at him like this throughout the whole night, and just imprinting, imprinting, imprinting. And then, until that imprinture was gone, and then I would stop painting. And I did this over a period of a couple of months or whatever, and then finished the painting. Because I finally got what I was looking for and what I needed to show. And I was very excited for him to see the painting.

So we brought him over one night, drove him down to that area. I had it covered with a sheet, and took the sheet off, and he just took it in. Didn't say a word for so long. And finally, I was standing next to him, and then I just went back to where Sherril was sitting on the bed, 'cause it was one of those places with just one room. It was, you know, the bed was in one corner and the painting was here . . . I just sat there, and he just stood there, forever. And . . . and this goes back to what we were just talking about, this kind of thing where you get credit for doing certain things when you have no consciousness of doing it anyway. But in my painting I have certain areas where

217

there are, where I've painted circles. And they're in certain kind of shape, in shapes, these several circles live in these various shapes. I did it because, I just wanted to experiment with color, and lightness, and everything that Brian and the music he was doing at the time meant to me. And then of course I wanted to show this kind of crazy person in the midst of all this stuff.

Well, apparently about that time Brian was very much into numerology. Well apparently each one of these little sections had X amount of circles in them, all adding up to a certain kind of numerological history of his life, and his dad's, and his – you know what I mean? It was all, it was eleven in this and nine in that, and seven in this and the seven were next to the nine, and all these kinds of things were going on. And I think the combination of that, and maybe just the fact of looking at himself in this painting . . . Um, he turned and he said, you know, the American Indian thing, "You've stolen my spirit, you've stolen my soul, captured my self."

And that was that. And that was *that*. I mean, from that point on things got strange with Brian and I. And then he got strange, and then it was very soon after that that I went up there with the lawyers one day and Brian wouldn't come out of the bedroom, and I just told Marilyn, this is it, I'm through, I'm finished. And I was gonna actually give Marilyn the painting, as a gift for Brian . . . and I still have it, I couldn't do that. I was too afraid to give it to her. PAUL: Yeah. No, it's appropriate, because he'd expressed that he was afraid of it. DAVID: Yeah. Blew me away. I was not expecting that.

PAUL: There's a lovely moment . . . of course, you've seen the documentary? DAVID: Mm-hm. PAUL: And I have to go back and see exactly what it was, but there's a moment near the end that I really like – and I like the whole film, I think it's wonderful – where Brian mentions his fears. He just shares, very openly, how the big thing for him is that he'll just get scared. He just says that in a way that really communicated to me, I forget the context, in the documentary, and I get the truth of it, and of course the story you're telling is around the same time that Jules's wife Cissy, although earlier, was banned from the house because Brian decided she was a witch. DAVID: [laughs] Yes. [Slaps his leg] I remember that. PAUL: And the point is that it is sincere, too. That is, the fear that he felt, when he looked at your painting, was real. It may not make sense to anybody, but he was dealing with his own fear, and in a sense you could even extend it, despite all the stuff about the numerology, you could even extend it to a compliment. That it's like, if you really *have* painted an effective . . . I mean, you saw Brian, as in the conversation that we had, as an absolutely extraordinary person. And so, if you have captured that, as you would want to, in your painting, then that you could understand is going to scare him.

DAVID: Well, you know what, in hindsight, after that experience and then with a little bit of time gone by after that . . . I mean, the fact of the matter is, whether I was conscious of it or not, he is mad in that painting. He is a madman in that painting. And I think that I did capture that madness, and I think that's maybe what I was after, and maybe that's what scared him. Although I didn't see it at the time, because I was obsessed with that whole other kind of vision that I thought I was doing . . . I mean I look at it *now*, it's hanging in the living room, and I can go and look at it now and I see the madness there. [laughs] I'm surprised he didn't turn around and shoot me, to be honest with you.

PAUL: Yeah, I mean I think that there have been times in any of our lives when it would be truly scary to really look in the mirror. But at least, you know, you can say, well . . .

DAVID: But you say what you said . . . now you say what you said about, you know, your feeling guilty about maybe you created the – You know, I could do the same thing. I could look at that painting and say, "You know what, this experience, his experience of that painting was very soon to the point at which he went crazy." And maybe, you know, he saw something in it that scared the pee out of him. About himself. But I'm not

219

going there, I'm sorry. You can go there if you want, but I'm not going. Heh.

PAUL: That's the thing. Look, if you've got a cut on your face and you don't know it, it may be a deep cut, it's going to make a difference the moment that you pass a store window and you actually see it, everything's gonna change. You see what I mean? It's that you know, and I know, that Brian was absolutely extraordinarily powerful, that's what you were talking about in the first part of the interview, at that time, and mad in a gorgeous, wonderful way – DAVID: Yeah. PAUL: So whatever, and it doesn't have to have been just that one moment with the painting but it could have been, but each moment at which he actually caught sight of himself . . . To me, I totally identify with that scaring him. I think that that could happen to any of us when we actually see, at a moment in our lives, how mad and powerful, and whatever, we really are; it's like we get by by hiding it from ourselves.

DAVID: I did a painting of Bob Dylan also at one time, and in that one I really was after something. And the first and only time Albert Grossman ever came over to my house, one afternoon, that painting was hanging up and he was sitting in a chair facing the wall that the painting was at. And this was like just before the "Dear Landlord" time . . . PAUL: Ah yes. DAVID: And this was another one of those weird things. I had given the painting to my friend Abe Sommers, and he had it in his apartment, because there was a time that maybe he was going to become the lawyer for Bob or something, Bob Dylan was going to come by his house. I really wanted Dylan to see this painting. Billy James wanted it to be a cover of one of the Dylan albums, he was still at CBS at the time. And so I was moving this painting around trying to position it so that, you know, it would be somewhere where Dylan might have a chance to see it. And it never happened, so I took it from Abe, I took it one night we got really high in his apartment, and he passed out and I took the painting, when I left I just took the painting off the wall and took it home. And put it on the wall.

Well, as things would have it, very soon after that Grossman is at my house, and I'll never forget, I'm sitting on the couch talking to him about some stuff, and he just could not deal with that painting. He had to get up and move so that he didn't have to see that painting. PAUL: Ohhh . . . DAVID: Which I loved! I thought it was great. And soon after that was the break-up with him and Bob, but I didn't know that was going on at the time . . .

PAUL: Well it seems to me, for what it's worth, that you might have had the same experience as Brian. That seeing how powerful your paintings really were – DAVID: I stopped painting. [laughs] I stopped painting. Oh well, whatever.

PAUL: I think this is how it works for us. I mean that it's really, it's genuinely terrifying, whether like Brian we notice the fear, or not. But to actually discover how powerful we are as individuals, or as creative individuals . . . DAVID: I think of that a lot. I do think of that a lot. I remember times people would say to me things like, you know, "Don't look at me like that." You know what I mean? And there are times I'll purpose-fully not do that. Because you're not conscious of it, or maybe we are, though . . .

I actually have a photograph over there somewhere of the drummer from the Smithreens standing next to the Brian painting. It was almost for a while, like one of those things like, when I started meeting people they would want to come to the house and see the painting and be photographed with it! And then send me the picture, which is really weird . . . PAUL: Wow. Again, it's like an American Indian thing. It is a totem, a power object . . . [laughter] CINDY: Yeah. It really draws people. DAVID: Well, it's all your fault anyway, Paul, if you wouldn't have written those interviews, none of this would have happened. I could have had a much quieter life, believe me! I'd have no Steven Gaines [Beach Boys biographer] in my life for months . . . PAUL: Oh God. Right.

I think that because Brian is so sensitive, because he does *feel* so much, that just even intuitively to feel that kind of responsibility, you know, for touching so many people . . . My own personal belief is, the ways we deal with our power shape our lives. And when we're talking about Bob Dylan or Brian Wilson, we are talking about people whom I regard as having great power. A fact of life is that that power in us actually scares us. That's natural. And we have to come to terms with that somehow.

20

The Beach Boys Love You and *Spring*

Always come back to the music. The artist matters because of what we experience when we're hearing his music. And what I want to say in this closing shot is, if the artist in question is Brian Wilson, these two albums, *The Beach Boys Love You* (1977) and *Spring* (1972), are important and rewarding (and mysteriously overlooked) works, vessels, music containers, to come back to again and again. Why? There's a lot of love, and a lot of craft and invention, in them. Good music. *Very* good music, measured by what this listener experiences when he hears it. Two beacons shining in what I've called the "wilderness" era, the seventeen years between the Beach Boys' *Surf's Up* album and *Brian Wilson*, the 1988 solo album. *Love You* and *Spring* may not be the stuff of legend, and they certainly have never been big sellers. But I like to think they'll be remembered anyway as major works by this great (and eccentric) artist. And I regret that neither album is currently in print in any format in the United States. I know the music world loves Brian Wilson. But why don't we give the guy more respect when he does what he does best?

What does he do? He almost said it himself, in chapter 17. He makes records that "give us strength and power." When we play them. If we can find them.

He tells the truth about his feelings in a deeply contemplative and imaginative musical language.

He does this sometimes through his voice and often through the voices of others (as well as through the voices of musical instruments). And the voices he's worked with the most other than those of the Beach Boys are those of his ex-wife and ex-sister-in-law, Marilyn Wilson and Diane Rovell, the Honeys, aka American Spring, aka Spring. Brian Wilson began producing the Beach Boys and the Honeys in 1963; and everything he did for the Beach Boys turned to gold for the next three years, and everything he did for the Honeys (five singles in the '60s and the Spring album in '71–72 and a few more tracks the next year) turned to nothing, no hits. Not for lack of effort on Brian's part nor for lack of talent on the part of the Rovell sisters and others who came and went from the group. But you can't win the lottery every time.

I do want to call the reader's attention to the fact that the story of Brian Wilson and the Beach Boys is partly a story about winning the lottery (when they had a great string of top ten records, 1962–66). We have a tendency to think of rock and roll (and pop music) as a meritocracy, where the successful and famous have power because their work is so good. Sometimes being good does have something to do with it, of course, but luck and timing also play a big part in most music success stories. So the pitfall for us is to assume that the difference between winners and losers (i.e., the "alternative" bands or rap artists you've heard of and those you haven't heard of) must be related to merit. Maybe sometimes. But my personal history of rock and roll is full of superb records (and artists) whose number didn't come up.

Brian Wilson had a great talent for working with the God-given voices of his brothers and cousin and family friend. This same talent (a kind of inspired creativity, arising from his sensitivity to the person's character and the person's voice and the sound of that person's voice in a recording studio or in combination with other voices and sounds) can also be heard in his work with his wife and sister-and-law. Found poetry. He found angels in his everyday life, and created works of lasting beauty out of the beauty he heard and saw in them. (I read somewhere, long ago, that the first working title of *Smile, Dumb*

Angel, was an expression of Brian's insight into the character of his brother Dennis.)

Let's start, once again, with "This Whole World." Words and music by Brian, sung by Carl on *Sunflower* in 1970, sung by Brian for *I Just Wasn't Made for These Times* in 1994, and sung by Marilyn in 1971 for *Spring,* with additional vocals by Diane Rovell and David Sandler, vocal arrangement by Brian Wilson. I don't know what more anyone could want from Brian Wilson than these three productions of this song (two as producer/arranger, one as performer). This (the *Spring* version, and don't settle for less than all three) is your dreamed-of *Smile*-level of creativity and complexity, except this time it's been stuck together. With affection, and lots of new ideas a year and a half after the excellent Beach Boys version. This *Spring* production of "This Whole World" is as inventive and as ahead-of-its-time as "I Get Around." This is the genius at work. Listen. Listen carefully. Listen to that extraordinary round in the new "Star light, star bright" section, modestly slipped in but comparable to the ending of "God Only Knows." Looking for Brian? Listen here. And what terrific performances he gets from Marilyn and Diane! And how about the way the instrumental track heats up in the last 20 seconds before the fade (the "And when I go anywhere" reprise)? What has been condensed into three minutes here is remarkable, really a nice taste of the kind of musical confection that was being reached for at the *Smile* moment. So much happens (and recurs) inside these three minutes! And this is the long version of "This Whole World" – the other two are under two minutes. The double vocal also serves to take the song into new realms of expressiveness. In terms of talking-about-feelings, this is the *Pet Sounds* side of Brian Wilson. Some of the best lyrics he ever wrote himself. And so subtle and artful and earnest! "Different kinds of people are the same." He says it, or induces Diane to say it, like a revelation. Legitimately, the song is a narrative about the speaker's awakening. Strange, in this case, that the patented Brian Wilson fret ("Still I Dream of It") about the pain of being a vulnerable male at the mercy of powerful females ("When they leave, you wait alone") is actually sung by female voices. (The voices, indeed, of the songwriter's wife and sometime paramour.) What does it all mean? A lot. A hell of a lot. And it's a genuine thing of beauty. "I see love . . ." Three minutes to explore and relive over and over. This is why we appreciate inspired music so much. And this is where you can find it.

Lots of it. Not just on "This Whole World" but on every track of this wonderful album. The voices are great. The music is thrilling. This is Brian Wilson at the top of his form, and I have to marvel that it's still such a well-kept secret after twenty-five years. Oh well, it took the world longer than that to notice *Moby Dick* or Van Gogh's paintings . . .

And look, it's okay with me if you don't appreciate *Spring* and *The Beach Boys Love You* as much as I do. But I do want to alert you (dear world, dear reader) to the possibility that your awe at some of what this artist has created could be an obstacle to noticing and enjoying the wondrous nature of much of his less-heralded output. In the previous chapter, David Anderle and I found ourselves announcing (or praying) that Brian is now free of *Smile* and other expectations created by his various accomplishments. And this isn't just about the artist. We the listeners and observers and appreciators of the artist's work can also in a sense be set free to "create" (discover) more of his great work by letting go of our attachment to the expectations we brought to *Wild Honey* or *Spring* or *Love You* or *I Just Wasn't Made for These Times* . . . Great art isn't just created by the genius of the artist. It's also created by the openness and receptivity of the individual reader, listener, observer. Yeah, but how can you expect me to enjoy a Beach Boys song if it's not about surf or cars???

"These things are me until I die." The point is, or could be, that when you die by letting go of seeing yourself as a cork on the ocean you can be reborn as a rock in a landslide or a leaf on a windy day. So how deep is the ocean then? Very deep indeed. Surf's up. Dive in.

Switching briefly to *The Beach Boys Love You*, which is, dear reader, another magnificently expressive musical opus when you open your heart to it, here's Brian's comment (to Timothy White in 1977) on how he wrote side two, track one, "Solar System":

"It just happened. I was on the way to a school meeting for my daughter. We went down there and on the way, in the car, I started thinking about, 'What do the planets mean?' I looked up in the sky and I saw the planets and I just thought, 'Hey! What do the planets mean to you? And have you ever seen the sunrise in the morning, shining like when you were born?' It's just something that came to my mind. Later on, I developed it into the song; I didn't come up with the title that night, but I wrote the words in the car."

Oh, friend, there's so much I want to tell you about what "Tennessee Waltz" and "Johnny Carson" and "Sweet Mountain" and "The Night Was So Young" and "Mona" and all the other wonders on these two albums mean to me. It's April 1997, and Brian's in his home studio in Chicago. Making music we might someday hear. But there's lots of music he's already made waiting cheerfully to be discovered. So I'll just tell you that these albums, track by track and taken as a whole, fill me with feelings I want to share. That's how deep the ocean is. Go thou and listen.

Appendix

Checklist of Beach Boys and Brian Wilson albums and singles

The Singles (both sides and date of first release)
all by the Beach Boys unless otherwise indicated

Surfin'/Luau   11/61
Barbie/What Is A Young Girl Made Of?
   (released under the name Kenney and the Cadets)   3/62
Surfin' Safari/409   6/62
Ten Little Indians/County Fair   11/62
Surfin' USA/Shut Down   3/63
Surfer Girl/Little Deuce Coupe   7/63
Be True to Your School/In My Room   10/63
Little Saint Nick/The Lord's Prayer   12/63
Pamela Jean/After the Game
     (released under the name The Survivors)   1/64
Fun, Fun, Fun/Why Do Fools Fall in Love?   2/64
I Get Around/Don't Worry Baby   5/64
When I Grow Up (to Be a Man)/She Knows Me Too Well
    8/64
Dance Dance Dance/The Warmth of the Sun   10/64
The Man with All the Toys/Blue Christmas   11/64
Do You Wanna Dance?/Please Let Me Wonder   2/65
Help Me, Rhonda/Kiss Me Baby   4/65
California Girls/Let Him Run Wild   7/65
The Little Girl I Once Knew/There's No Other
    (Like My Baby)   11/65

Barbara Ann/Girl, Don't Tell Me   12/65
Caroline, No/Summer Means New Love
    (Brian Wilson solo single)   3/66
Sloop John B/You're So Good to Me   3/66
Wouldn't It Be Nice/God Only Knows   7/66
Good Vibrations/Let's Go Away for Awhile   10/66
Heroes and Villains/You're Welcome   7/67
Gettin' Hungry/Devoted to You
    (released as "by Brian Wilson and Mike Love")   9/67
Wild Honey/Wind Chimes   10/67
Darlin'/Here Today   12/67
Friends/Little Bird   4/68
Do It Again/Wake the World   7/68
Bluebirds over the Mountain/Never Learn Not to Love
    12/68
Break Away/Celebrate the News   6/69
Add Some Music to Your Day/Susie Cincinnati   2/70
Cotton Fields/The Nearest Faraway Place   4/70
Slip on Through/This Whole World   6/70
Tears in the Morning/It's About Time   10/70
Cool Cool Water/Forever   3/71
Long Promised Road/Deirdre   5/71
Long Promised Road/'Til I Die   10/71
Surf's Up/Don't Go Near the Water   11/71
You Need A Mess of Help to Stand Alone/Cuddle Up   5/72
Marcella/Hold On, Dear Brother   6/72
Sail On, Sailor/Only with You   2/73
California Saga/Funky Pretty   4/73
Child of Winter & Here Comes Santa Claus/Susie Cincinnati
    12/74
Rock and Roll Music/TM Song   5/76
It's O.K./Had to Phone Ya   8/76
Graduation Day/Be True to Your School   9/76
Susie Cincinnati/Everyone's in Love with You   11/76
Honkin' Down the Highway/Solar System   5/77
Peggy Sue/Hey, Little Tomboy   8/78

Here Comes the Night/Baby Blue   2/79
Good Timin'/Love Surrounds Me   4/79
Lady Lynda/Full Sail   8/79
It's a Beautiful Day/Sumahama   10/79
Goin' On/Endless Harmony   3/80
Livin' with a Heartache/Santa Ana Winds   5/80
The Beach Boys Medley/God Only Knows   7/81
East Meets West (with Frankie Valli and the Four Seasons)
     1984
Getcha Back/Male Ego   4/85
It's Gettin Late/It's OK   1985
She Believes in Love Again   1985
Rock 'n' Roll to the Rescue/Good Vibrations   1986
California Dreamin'   1986
Happy Endings (with Little Richard)/California Girls   1987
Wipe Out (with the Fat Boys)   1987
Let's Go to Heaven in My Car/Too Much Sugar
     (Brian Wilson solo)   1987
Love and Mercy/He Couldn't Get His Poor Old Body to Move
     (Brian Wilson solo)   7/88
Kokomo   9/88
Don't Worry Baby (with the Everly Brothers)   1989
Melt Away/Being with the One You Love
     (Brian Wilson solo)   1989
Still Cruisin'/Kokomo   1989
Somewhere Near Japan   1989
Problem Child   1990
Crocodile Rock   1991
Hot Fun in the Summertime/Summer in Love   1992
Summer in Love   1995
Do It Again/'Til I Die/This Song Wants to Sleep with You
     Tonight (Brian Wilson solo)   1995
Fun, Fun, Fun (with Status Quo)   3/96
Little Deuce Coupe (with James House)   1996
I Can Hear Music (with Kathy Troccoli)   1996
Don't Worry Baby (with Lorrie Morgan)   1996

The Albums (title, date of first release, and track names)
(all but the two best-known compilation albums have been omitted from this checklist)
(all by the Beach Boys unless otherwise indicated)

Surfin' Safari 10/62
Surfin' Safari/County Fair/Ten Little Indians/Chug-a-Lug/
Little Girl (You're My Miss America)/409/Surfin'/Heads You
Win – Tails I Lose/Summertime Blues/Cuckoo Clock/Moon
Dawg/The Shift

Surfin' U.S.A. 3/63
Surfin' U.S.A./Farmer's Daughter/Misirlou/Stoked/Lonely
Sea/Shut Down/Noble Surfer/Honky Tonk/Lana/Surf Jam/
Let's Go Trippin'/Finders Keepers

Surfer Girl 9/63
Surfer Girl/Catch a Wave/The Surfer Moon/South Bay
Surfer/The Rocking Surfer/Little Deuce Coupe/In My
Room/Hawaii/Surfer's Rule/Our Car Club/Your Summer
Dream/Boogie Woodie

Little Deuce Coupe 10/63
Little Deuce Coupe/Ballad of Ole ' Betsy/Be True to Your
School/Car Crazy Cutie/Cherry, Cherry Coupe/409/Shut
Down/Spirit of America/Our Car Club/No-Go Showboat/A
Young Man Is Gone/Custom Machine

Shut Down, Vol. 2 3/64
Fun, Fun, Fun/Don't Worry Baby/In the Parking Lot/"Cas-
sius" Love Vs. "Sonny" Wilson/The Warmth of the Sun/This
Car of Mine/Why Do Fools Fall in Love/Pom Pom Play Girl/
Keep an Eye on Summer/Shut Down, Part 2/Louie, Louie/
Denny's Drums

All Summer Long   7/64

I Get Around/All Summer Long/Hushabye/Little Honda/ We'll Run Away/Carl's Big Chance/Wendy/Do You Remember?/Girls on the Beach/Drive-In/Our Favorite Recording Sessions/Don't Back Down

Beach Boys Christmas Album   10/64

Little Saint Nick/The Man with All the Toys/Santa's Beard/Merry Christmas Baby/Christmas Day/Frosty the Snowman/We Three Kings of Orient Are/Blue Christmas/ Santa Claus Is Comin' to Town/White Christmas/I'll Be Home for Christmas/Auld Lang Syne

Beach Boys Concert   10/64

Fun, Fun, Fun/The Little Old Lady from Pasadena/ Little Deuce Coupe/Long Tall Texan/In My Room/The Monster Mash/Let's Go Trippin'/Papa-Oom-Mow-Mow/The Wanderer/Hawaii/Graduation Day/I Get Around/Johnny B. Goode

The Beach Boys Today!   3/65

Do You Wanna Dance?/Good to My Baby/Don't Hurt My Little Sister/When I Grow Up (to Be a Man)/Help Me, Rhonda/Dance, Dance, Dance/Please Let Me Wonder/I'm So Young/Kiss Me, Baby/She Knows Me Too Well/In the Back of My Mind/Bull Session with "Big Daddy"

Summer Days (and Summer Nights!!)   7/65

The Girl from New York City/Amusement Parks U.S.A./Then I Kissed Her/Salt Lake City/Girl, Don't Tell Me/Help Me, Rhonda/California Girls/Let Him Run Wild/You're So Good to Me/Summer Means New Love/I'm Bugged at My Old Man/ And Your Dream Comes True

Beach Boys Party! 11/65
Hully Gully/I Should Have Known Better/Tell Me Why/Papa-Oom-Mow-Mow/Mountain of Love/You've Got to Hide Your Love Away/Devoted to You/Alley Oop/There's No Other (Like My Baby)/Medley: I Get Around, Little Deuce Coupe/The Times They Are A-Changin'/Barbara Ann

Pet Sounds 5/66
Wouldn't It Be Nice/You Still Believe in Me/That's Not Me/Don't Talk (Put Your Head on My Shoulder)/I'm Waiting for the Day/Let's Go Away for Awhile/Sloop John B./God Only Knows/I Know There's An Answer/Here Today/I Just Wasn't Made For These Times/Pet Sounds/Caroline, No

Smiley Smile 9/67
Heroes and Villains/Vegetables/Fall Breaks and Back to Winter (W. Woodpecker Symphony)/She's Goin' Bald/Little Pad/Good Vibrations/With Me Tonight/Wind Chimes/Gettin' Hungry/Wonderful/Whistle In

Wild Honey 12/67
Wild Honey/Aren't You Glad/I Was Made to Love Her/Country Air/A Thing or Two/Darlin'/I'd Love Just Once to See You/Here Comes the Night/Let the Wind Blow/How She Boogalooed It/Mama Says

Friends 6/68
Meant for You/Friends/Wake the World/Be Here in the Morning/When a Man Needs a Woman/Passing By/Anna Lee, the Healer/Little Bird/Be Still/Busy Doin' Nothin'/Diamond Head/Transcendental Meditation

Stack-o-Tracks 8/68
Darlin'/Salt Lake City/Sloop John B/In My Room/Catch a Wave/Wild Honey/Little Saint Nick/Do It Again/Wouldn't It Be Nice/God Only Knows/Surfer Girl/Little Honda/Here Today/You're So Good to Me/Let Him Run Wild

20/20 2/69
Do It Again/I Can Hear Music/Bluebirds Over the Mountain/
Be with Me/All I Want to Do/The Nearest Faraway Place/
Cotton Fields/I Went to Sleep/Time to Get Alone/Never
Learn Not to Love/Our Prayer/Cabinessence

Live in London 5/70
Darlin'/Wouldn't It Be Nice/Sloop John B/California Girls/
Do It Again/Wake the World/Aren't You Glad/Bluebirds
Over the Mountain/Their Hearts Were Full of Spring/Good
Vibrations/God Only Knows/Barbara Ann

Sunflower 8/70
Slip on Through/This Whole World/Add Some Music to Your
Day/Got to Know the Woman/Deirdre/It's About Time/Tears
in the Morning/All I Wanna Do/Forever/Our Sweet Love/At
My Window/Cool, Cool Water

Surf's Up 8/71
Don't Go Near the Water/Long Promised Road/Take a Load
Off Your Feet/Disney Girls (1957)/Student Demonstration
Time/Feel Flows/Lookin' at Tomorrow (A Welfare Song)/A
Day in the Life of a Tree/'Til I Die/Surf's Up

Carl and the Passions – So Tough 5/72
You Need a Mess of Help to Stand Alone/Here She Comes/
He Come Down/Marcella/Hold On, Dear Brother/Make It
Good/All This Is That/Cuddle Up

Spring (by Spring, produced & arranged by Brian Wilson with
David Sandler) 7/72
Tennessee Waltz/Thinkin' Bout You Baby/Mama Said/
Superstar/Awake/Sweet Mountain/Everybody/This Whole
World/Forever/Good Time/Now That Everything's Been
Said/Down Home

Holland   1/73
Sail On Sailor/Steamboat/California Saga (Big Sur, The Beaks of Eagles, California)/The Trader/Leaving This Town/Only with You/Funky Pretty/Mount Vernon and Fairway

The Beach Boys in Concert   11/73
Sail on Sailor/Sloop John B/The Trader/You Still Believe in Me/California Girls/Darlin'/Marcella/Caroline, No/Leaving This Town/Heroes and Villains/Funky Pretty/Let the Wind Blow/Help Me, Rhonda/Surfer Girl/Wouldn't It Be Nice/We Got Love/Don't Worry Baby/Surfin' U.S.A./Good Vibrations/Fun, Fun, Fun

Endless Summer   6/74
Surfin' Safari/Surfer Girl/Catch a Wave/The Warmth of the Sun/Surfin' U.S.A./Be True to Your School/Little Deuce Coupe/In My Room/Shut Down/Fun, Fun, Fun/I Get Around/Girls on the Beach/Wendy/Let Him Run Wild/Don't Worry Baby/California Girls/Girl Don't Tell Me/Help Me, Rhonda/You're So Good to Me/All Summer Long

15 Big Ones   7/76
Rock and Roll Music/It's O.K./Had to Phone Ya/Chapel of Love/Everyone's in Love with You/Medley: Talk to Me, Tallahassee Lassie/That Same Song/TM Song/Palisades Park/Susie Cincinnati/A Casual Look/Blueberry Hill/Back Home/In the Still of the Night/Just Once in My Life

The Beach Boys Love You   4/77
Let Us Go On This Way/Roller Skating Child/Mona/Johnny Carson/Good Time/Honkin' Down the Highway/Ding Dang/Solar System/The Night Was So Young/I'll Bet He's Nice/Let's Put Our Hearts Together/I Wanna Pick You Up/Airplane/Love Is a Woman

M.I.U. Album 9/78
She's Got Rhythm/Come Go with Me/Hey, Little Tomboy/
Kona Coast/Peggy Sue/Wontcha Come Out Tonight?/Sweet
Sunday Kinda Love/Belles of Paris/Pitter Patter/My Diane/
Match Point of Our Love/Winds of Change

L.A. (Light Album) 3/79
Good Timin'/Lady Lynda/Full Sail/Angel Come Home/
Love Surrounds Me/Sumahama/Here Comes the Night/Baby
Blue/Goin' South/Shortenin' Bread

Keepin' the Summer Alive 3/80
Keepin' the Summer Alive/Oh, Darlin'/Some of Your Love/
Livin' with a Heartache/School Days/Goin' On/Sunshine/
When Girls Get Together/Santa Ana Winds/Endless Harmony

The Beach Boys 7/85
Getcha Back/It's Gettin' Late/Crack at Your Love/Maybe I
Don't Know/She Believes in Love Again/California Calling/
Passing Friend/I'm So Lonely/Where I Belong/I Do Love
You/It's Just a Matter of Time

Brian Wilson (solo album) 6/88
Love and Mercy/Walkin' the Line/Melt Away/Baby Let your
Hair Grow Long/Little Children/One for the Boys/There's
So Many/Night Time/Let It Shine/Meet Me in My Dreams
Tonight/Rio Grande

Still Cruisin' 8/89
Still Cruisin'/Somewhere Near Japan/Island Girl/In My Car/
Kokomo/Wipe Out/Make It Big/I Get Around/Wouldn't It
Be Nice/California Girls

Summer in Paradise 8/92
Hot Fun in the Summertime/Surfin'/Summer of Love/Island
Fever/Still Surfin'/Medley: Slow Summer Dancin', One Sum-
mer Night/Strange Things Happen/Remember (Walkin' in
the Sand)/Lahaina Aloha/Under the Boardwalk/Summer in
Paradise/Forever

Good Vibrations, 30 Years of the Beach Boys   6/93

disc 1: Surfin' U.S.A./Little Surfer Girl/Surfin'/Surfin'/ Their Hearts Were Full of Spring/Surfin' Safari/409/ Punchline/Surfin' U.S.A./Shut Down/Surfer Girl/Little Deuce Coupe/In My Room/Catch a Wave/The Surfer Moon/Be True to Your School/Spirit of America/Little Saint Nick/Things We Did Last Summer/Fun, Fun, Fun/ Don't Worry Baby/Why Do Fools Fall in Love/The Warmth of the Sun/I Get Around/All Summer Long/Little Honda/ Wendy/Don't Back Down/Do You Wanna Dance/When I Grow Up (to Be a Man)/Dance, Dance, Dance/Please Let Me Wonder/She Knows Me Too Well/Radio Station Jingles/concert promo + Hushabye

disc 2: California Girls/Help Me, Rhonda/Then I Kissed Her/And Your Dreams Come True/The Little Girl I Once Knew/Barbara Ann/Ruby Baby/radio promo spot/Sloop John B/Wouldn't It Be Nice/You Still Believe in Me/God Only Knows/Hang On to Your Ego/I Just Wasn't Made for These Times/Pet Sounds/Caroline, No/Good Vibrations/ Our Prayer/Heroes and Villains/Heroes and Villains (sections)/Wonderful/Cabinessence/Wind Chimes/Heroes and Villains (intro)/Do You Like Worms/Vegetables/I Love to Say Da Da/Surf's Up/With Me Tonight

disc 3: Heroes and Villains/Darlin'/Wild Honey/Let the Wind Blow/Can't Wait Too Long/Cool Cool Water/Meant for You/Friends/Little Bird/Busy Doin' Nothin'/Do It Again/I Can Hear Music/I Went to Sleep/Time to Get Alone/Break Away/Cotton Fields (The Cotton Song)/San Miguel/Games Two Can Play/I Just Got My Pay/This Whole World/Add Some Music/Forever/Our Sweet Love/H.E.L.P. Is on the Way/4th of July/Long Promised Road/Disney Girls/Surf's Up/'Til I Die disc 4: Sail On Sailor/California/Trader/Funky Pretty/Fairy Tale Music/You Need a Mess of Help to Stand Alone/ Marcella/All This Is That/Rock and Roll Music/It's OK/Had to Phone Ya/That Same Song/It's Over Now/Still I Dream of It/Let Us Go On This Way/The Night Was So Young/I'll Bet He's Nice/Airplane/Come Go with Me/Our Team/Baby Blue/Good Timin'/Goin' On/Getcha Back/Kokomo

disc 5: In My Room (demo)/radio spot/I Get Around (track only)/radio spot/Dance, Dance, Dance (tracking session)/Hang On to Your Ego (sessions)/God Only Knows (tracking session)/Good Vibrations (sessions)/Heroes and Villains (track only)/Cabinessence (track only)/Surf's Up (track only)/radio spot/All Summer Long (vocals)/Wendy (vocals)/Hushabye (vocals)/When I Grow Up (to Be a Man) (vocals)/Wouldn't It Be Nice (vocals)/California Girls (vocals)/radio spot/concert intro + Surfin' U.S.A. (live 1964)/Surfer Girl (live 1964)/Be True to Your School (live 1964)/Good Vibrations (live 1966)/Surfer Girl (live in Hawaii rehearsals, 1967)

"I Just Wasn't Made for These Times" (Brian Wilson solo album/ soundtrack)   8/95
Meant for You/This Whole World/Caroline, No/Let the Wind Blow/Love and Mercy/Do It Again/The Warmth of the Sun/ Wonderful/Still I Dream of It/Melt Away/'Til I Die

Orange Crate Art (by Brian Wilson and Van Dyke Parks)   11/95
Orange Crate Art/Sail Away/My Hobo Heart/Wings of a Dove/Palm Tree and Moon/Summer in Monterey/San Francisco/Hold Back Time/My Jeanine/Movies Is Magic/This Town Goes Down at Sunset/Lullaby

Stars and Stripes, Vol. I   8/96
Don't Worry Baby (with Lorrie Morgan)/Little Deuce Coupe
(with James House)/409 (with Junior Brown)/Long Tall
Texan (with Doug Supernaw)/I Get Around (with Sawyer
Brown)/Be True to Your School (with Toby Keith)/Fun, Fun,
Fun (with Ricky Van Shelton/Help Me, Rhonda (with T.
Graham Brown)/The Warmth of the Sun (with Willie
Nelson)/Sloop John B. (with Collin Raye)/I Can Hear Music
(with Kathy Troccoli)/Caroline, No (with Timothy B. Schmit)